NATIONAL
GEOGRAPHIC

Atlas

OF THE

Middle East

SECOND EDITION

Growth of Major Cities

Total Population   Year

7,000,000 — 2010
6,000,000 —
5,000,000 — 1980
4,000,000 —
3,000,000 —
2,000,000 —
1,000,000 — 1950
0 —

*Map shows all cities with
a population of at least
750,000 by the year 2010.*

Istanbul

Bursa

Izmir

Ankara

Konya

Adana

Gaziantep

Halab

Homs

CYPRUS

Beirut

Damascus

SYRIA

Mosul

Arbil

Baghdad

IRAQ

Haifa

Tel Aviv-Yafo

ISRAEL

Amman

JORDAN

T U R K E Y

Alexandria

Cairo

E G Y P T

Medina

SAUD

Jeddah

Mecca

Khartoum

S U D A N

Sanaa

Atlas
OF THE
Middle
East

SECOND EDITION

NATIONAL GEOGRAPHIC

WASHINGTON, DC

SHEIKH ZAYED ROAD, DUBAI, UNITED ARAB EMIRATES.
A towering new hub of the Middle East, Dubai is the crown jewel of the United Arab Emirates. Rising on the shores of the Persian Gulf, the city attracts businesses, wealthy new residents, and travelers — and poor guest workers from other Middle Eastern countries. Together, they've made Dubai one of the fastest growing cities in the world. Oil, discovered offshore in the 1970s, fueled the phenomenal growth, but those reserves are quickly dwindling. A real estate boom that has brought the city, among other things, the tallest building on the planet and an indoor ski slope accounts for its new moniker, "Mushroom City."

Contents

Black Gold, Black Plague

BY DON BELT

O NE HUNDRED YEARS AGO — on May 26, 1908, to be precise — a heavy-set, mustachioed British lawyer and mining entrepreneur named William Knox D'Arcy, drilling in the Zagros Mountains of western Persia, struck a giant pool of oil 1,200 feet below the surface of the Earth and changed our world forever. His pioneering discovery, along with others that followed in neighboring lands of Arabia and the Ottoman Empire, would reshape the destiny of the Middle East and bind its fortunes to the industrial-ized West, whose craving for petroleum — a twinge in 1908 — would soon become insatiable.

Over the past century, a gathering, undeclared war over oil has turned the Middle East of this atlas (expanded to include Afghanistan, Pakistan, and Sudan) into a geopoliti-cal chessboard and has magnified its struggles so that they have become the front-page narratives of our time. The Arab-Israeli conflict, the 1979 Iranian Islamic revolution, the Soviet invasion of Afghanistan, the Iran-Iraq war, the Persian Gulf war, the roots of al Qaeda, the horrors of 9/11, genocides in Sudan, and the ongoing war in Iraq — all have petroleum embedded in the story line. Even if the Middle East weren't the cradle of Judaism, Christianity, and Islam, it would still be at the center of our consciousness because of what it possesses: 65 percent of the world's known supply of oil.

Oil was certainly on the minds of Europe's politicians when the Ottoman Empire, an ally of Germany, fell at the end of World War I and the victors met to divide the spoils. Begin-ning in 1919, the victorious Allies of Europe (Great Britain, France, and Italy) divided Ottoman lands into spheres of influence and, drawing lines on a map, proceeded to fashion new European-ruled entities—Iraq, Transjordan, Lebanon, Syria, and Palestine (which its protec-tor, Britain, had committed to making a Jewish homeland in 1917). This made more sense to the European powers who coveted them than to the residents themselves, mostly Arabic-speaking Muslims whose identities derived not from some abstract sense of nationality but from their families, their tribes, and their faith.

Colonialism collapsed in the 1920s and '30s and died after World War II, when a rising tide of nationalism won independence for these artificial states and forged two new countries, Israel and Pakistan, as homelands for religious minorities. But with few exceptions, the secular rulers who came to power afterward turned out to be just as corrupt, despotic, and greedy as the imperialists they replaced—and less concerned with the needs of their citizens than with acquir-ing and hoarding power. As long as the oil continued to flow and "stability" was maintained, the West was usually quite supportive.

By the late 20th century, citizens of a few oil-rich nations had grown fabulously wealthy while the vast majority of Middle Easterners — overwhelmingly young, poor, and confined to desert lands scarce in resources — languished, falling further and further behind Western standards of education, technology, economic opportunity, freedom, and hope. Today, mil-lions of people in these societies have rejected the secular institutions that failed them and turned to "political" Islam, which began as an Egyptian anti-colonial movement in the 1920s

but made its breakthrough decades later, with the 1979 Islamic revolution in Iran.

Based on a return to fundamental Islamic principles and on the life of the Prophet Muhammad (A.D. 570-632), such movements are limited as a prescription for success in a globalized, 21st-century world. And they have inspired political extremists such as al Qaeda to justify savagery in the name of religion. But they have also given Muslims — who make up 92 percent of the region's population — a way to push back, to demand better, to reclaim the dignity and identity they've lost since the day Mr. D'Arcy struck oil.

STEPPING UP TO VOTE in their country's first ever presidential election in October 2004, burka-clad women — registration cards in hand — wait at a polling station in Kabul. Left in ruins by the Soviet Union's 1979 invasion, the anti-Soviet jihad of the 1980s, and the rise of the Taliban in the 1990s, Afghanistan is governed largely by tradition and tribal warlords and remains one of the poorest countries on Earth.

At the Crossroads

BY K. M. KOSTYAL

"Oh, East is East, and West is West, and never the twain shall meet," the writer Rudyard Kipling famously wrote. But he was wrong. The twain do meet in the Middle East, a region that for some 3,000 years has created a vibrant cultural stew, as well as an often conflicted, even dangerous suq of goods, ideas, and beliefs.

A land of nuance and subtlety, the Middle East remains ever elusive as an entity. Here, the obvious is not necessarily as it appears. Even the term Middle East is problematic. Before the New World was known to Europeans or Asians, Old World geographers saw the Earth as composed of the great world-island of Eurasia. With that as their perspective, "East" meant Asia and "West," Europe. In between lay the eastern Mediterranean and the swath that extends north to the Ural Mountains — today's Middle East. But during the 14th through the early 20th centuries, when the Ottoman Empire held sway, Europeans and Americans called the region the Near East — that is, nearer to them than the Far East lands of India, China, and Japan — but no less exotic.

THOUSANDS OF ANGRY YOUNG SHIITE MEN, followers of cleric Muqtada al-Sadr, gathered in 2003 to protest near the headquarters of the U.S.-led Coalition Provisional Authority in Najaf, a Shiite holy city (above). With the fall of Saddam Hussein, long-simmering tensions erupted between Iraq's Sunni and Shiite Muslims. The Sunni-Shiite divide dates almost to the inception of Islam, and today it again threatens to pull the Middle East apart. The deep past remains a vital part of the present in the region: In the desert of northeastern Sudan (right), 2,200-year-old pyramids still mark the royal necropolis of Meroe, constructed by the Kushite (Nubian) rulers who once dominated the region.

TRADITIONAL
MIDDLE EAST

CULTURAL
MIDDLE EAST

THE TRADITIONAL AND CULTURAL MIDDLE EASTS

The territory depicted on the top map reflects what historians and geographers have long considered the Middle East. The cultural Middle East, shown on the map below, extends beyond that, from south-central Asia to North Africa and the lands in between, all areas strongly influenced by Islam.

SATELLITE DISHES IN SYRIA

The skyscape of Halab, or Aleppo—Syria's largest city—blooms with a veritable roof garden of satellite dishes. With literacy rates still low throughout the Middle East, satellite TV has become the major source of news. The popular but controversial Al Jazeera news channel reaches 50 million viewers.

The people of the Middle East have never considered themselves either exotic or halfway to anything else. Rather, they have known they were at the center of it all—the literal and proverbial crossroads of cultures, in fact the birthplace of civilization itself. Here, almost 10,000 years ago, people developed agriculture, harvesting a surplus of grain that allowed humans for the first time to turn their attention to other pursuits beyond just feeding themselves. The lands of the Tigris and Euphrates Rivers, now so embroiled in the Iraqi conflict, gave rise to the earliest civilization, marked by the advent of artisans, craftsmen, merchants, cities for commerce, and an ability to record events, transactions, and history.

From Mesopotamia, the tools and techniques of civilization spread in a "fertile crescent" to Anatolia, today's Turkey, through Syria and into Egypt. While humans in what is now Europe still lived in rough huts in the forest, the Middle East spawned such elaborate empires as Sumeria, Babylonia, Assyria, and Persia. They raised cities replete with temples and terraces, irrigation systems, and highways. They produced legal codes, calendars, coinage, postal systems, bureaucrats, scribes, scholars—and religions. The ancient Egyptian civilization, spanning thousands of years, had an elaborate system of gods and goddesses. But the nomadic desert people in those millennia had their own beliefs, and the monotheistic convictions of one of the legendary wanderers, Abraham, gave rise to three great religions—Judaism, Christianity, and Islam. Still today, adherents of all three look to the Middle East as sacred land—their sacred land—and that, over the centuries, has led to interminable, seemingly irresolvable conflict. From the battles the Jews fought in the sixth century B.C. to protect their first temple in Jerusalem, to the Roman occupation in the centuries prior to and following the birth of Jesus, to the early struggles of Christians to establish their religion here, to the rise of Islam in the seventh century A.D., to the medieval Crusades fought by Europeans to take back the "Holy Land" for Christianity, to the conflicts of today, the Middle East has had a tortured history. War and violence have

ATLAS OF THE MIDDLE EAST,
SECOND EDITION COVERAGE

FEATURED AREA OF THIS ATLAS
Coverage includes the countries of the "traditional" Middle East, along with Sudan, Afghanistan, and Pakistan. This second edition of the atlas has been expanded to incorporate these countries, whose fates are vital to the stability of the Middle East and the world.

been and continue to be interwoven into the fabric of life. The protracted struggle between Palestinians and Israelis rages on, as does the less obvious but equally invidious struggle to control petroleum reserves. And the Muslim sphere, which has prevailed in the Middle East since the Bedouin cavalry of the Prophet Muhammad thundered out of the Arabian Peninsula almost 1,400 years ago, is now rent, with the Sunni and Shiite factions of Islam again vying with one another for dominance, as they have almost since the birth of the religion. Current geopolitics only exacerbates that struggle as the Persian/Shiite influence of Iran squares off with the traditional Sunni forces of such powerful Arab neighbors as Saudi Arabia.

This atlas follows the tensions and triumphs of an area like no other on Earth, explaining in the clearest terms who the national players in this ongoing drama are, what issues engage them, and the geography in this remarkable pocket of the planet that has inspired and motivated so many, from religious devotees to oil speculators. Covering in depth the traditional geographic Middle East — those nations and political entities that occupy the crucible of cultures between three continents, from Egypt to Iran and Turkey to Yemen — this second edition of the atlas also enlarges its coverage of the cultural, Islamic Middle East, which stretches from North Africa all the way to south-central Asia. Coverage of Afghanistan and Pakistan, steeped in the turbulence of the modern Middle East, is included in this new edition. The Sudan, ever in the news with its endless ethnic and land clashes generated by the Arab government in Khartoum toward the African peoples in the south and west, has also been added to provide you with a deeper understanding of that conflicted country.

In the months and years ahead, we hope this volume will serve as an enduring source of insight to you, as the Middle East continues to be — and it surely will — at the center of world events.

The Middle East in the World

Winkel Tripel Projection
SCALE 1:96,361,000
1 CENTIMETER = 963 KILOMETERS; 1 INCH = 1521 MILES AT THE EQUATOR

0 500 1000 1500 2000 2500
KILOMETERS

0 500 1000 1500 2000 2500
STATUTE MILES

Countries
and Cities

LEFT TO RIGHT: Security personnel of Palestinian President Mahmoud Abbas ("Force 17") perform a training routine in Ramallah, July 2007; Benazir Bhutto, Pakistan's former prime minister, holds up her party's 2008 manifesto during a news conference in Islamabad, November 2007, one month prior to her assassination; Quba Mosque, outside Medina, Saudi Arabia; Supporters of Iraq's team shout slogans during the final match (Iraq vs. Saudi Arabia) of the AFC Asian Cup, July 2007; Backdropped by the national flag, Israeli Prime Minister Ehud Olmert is seen at his Sukkah, on the occasion of the Jewish holiday of Sukkot (Feast of the Tabernacles) in Jerusalem.

Area and Latitude Comparison

Map Key

QATAR ——— Country
48–49 ——— Page numbers

0   400   800
KILOMETERS

0   400   800
STATUTE MILES

Lambert Azimuthal Equal-Area Projection

80° N
70° N
60° N
50° N
40° N
30° N
20° N
10° N

TURKEY 56–57

28–29 **CYPRUS**
42–43 **LEBANON**
36–37 **ISRAEL**

SYRIA 54–55

IRAQ 34–35

IRAN 32–33

AFGHANISTAN 24–25

PAKISTAN 46–47

OCCUPIED PALESTINIAN TERRITORIES 62–63

JORDAN 38–39

KUWAIT 40–41

EGYPT 30–31

BAHRAIN 26–27

QATAR 48–49

U.A.E. 58–59

OMAN 44–45

SAUDI ARABIA 50–51

SUDAN 52–53

YEMEN 60–61

Abbreviations

A.D. .... *In the year of the Lord*	°F .... *degrees Fahrenheit*	Rep. .... *Republic*
Af. .... *Africa*	GDP .... *Gross Domestic Product*	St. .... *Street*
AGR .... *Agriculture*	Gez. .... *Gezîret*	Str. .... *Strait*
Arm. .... *Armenia*	Gezr. .... *Gezâir*	Syr. .... *Syria*
Ave. .... *Avenue*	I.A.E.A. .... *International Atomic Energy Agency*	Terr. .... *Territories*
Avg. .... *Average*	IND .... *Industry*	Turk. .... *Turkey*
Azerb. .... *Azerbaijan*	L. .... *Lake*	U.A.E. .... *United Arab Emirates*
B.C. .... *Before Christ*	Leb. .... *Lebanon*	U.K. .... *United Kingdom*
°C .... *degrees Celsius (centigrade)*	Mt.-s. .... *Mount–ain–s*	U.N. .... *United Nations*
ca .... *circa*	Occ. Pal. Terr. .... *Occupied Palestinian Territories*	UNMOVIC .... *United Nations Monitoring, Verification, and Inspection Commission*
Cen. .... *Central*	Org. .... *Organization*	
Chan. .... *Channel*	Pen. .... *Peninsula*	UNSCOM .... *United Nations Special Commission*
Dem. .... *Democratic*	PLO .... *Palestine Liberation Organization*	U.S. .... *United States*
Eth. .... *Ethiopia*	Ra. .... *Range*	UTC .... *Coordinated Universal Time*
EXP .... *Exports*	Rd. .... *Road*	W. .... *Wadi, Wādī, Wâdi*

Key to the Country Maps

MAP SYMBOLS

- ✪ Capital
- ●●●● Cities
- ✈ Airport
- ⬦ Oil field
- ∴ Ruin
- ⌑ Point of interest
- *Aswan High Dam* ⌐ Dam
- ○ Water hole
- ⊙ Crater
- *Jabal Naba* ✛ Peak with elevation
  (Mt. Nebo) in meters
  802
- -154. Depression with elevation
  in meters
- 3003 ⤳ Pass with elevation
  in meters

HUMAN FEATURES

- .... International boundary
- .– .– .– De facto or undefined boundary
- .... Claimed boundary
- ━━━ Super highway
- – – – – Super highway under construction
- ——— Highway
- ——— Other road
- – – – – – Ferry
- |||||||||||| Canal
- •—•—•— Aqueduct
- •—•—•— Oil pipeline
- MESOPOTAMIA Historic or cultural region
- ▨ United Nations peacekeeping zone

NATURAL FEATURES

- ——— Perennial drainage
- ←– – – Intermittent drainage
- – – – – Indefinite coastline
- ⬍ Falls or rapids
- ㉙ Water surface elevation in meters
- ⬱ Area below sea level
- ⬭ Intermittent lake
- ⬭ Dry salt lake
- ⬭ Salt desert
- ▭ Marsh, swamp, or wetland
- ▭ Sand
- ▭ Lava

Note: City map symbols appear on page 65

Geographic Equivalents

Ab	*river, lake*	Gezîret	*island*	Kul	*lake*
'Ain	*spring, well*	Ghubbat	*bay, gulf*	Lac	*lake*
Arḍ	*area*	Gölü	*lake*	Masabb	*mouth of river*
Aylagy	*bay, gulf*	Gowd	*depression*	Mīnā'	*harbor*
Bāb	*gate, strait*	Haḍabat	*plateau*	Mukhayyam	*refugee camp*
Bahr	*river*	Ḥadd	*spit*	Nafūd	*area of dunes, desert*
Baḥr, Baḥra	*lake*	Ḥālat	*island*	Qā'	*depression, mudflat*
Bandar	*anchorage, bay, bight, port*	Hamun, Hāmūn	*lake, depression*	Qal'at	*fort*
Baraji	*dam, reservoir*	Har	*hill, mountain*	Qarn	*hill*
Baṭn	*depression, wadi*	Ḥarrat	*lava field*	Qaṣr	*castle, fort*
Be'er	*well*	Hawr	*lake, marsh*	Qiryat	*settlement, suburb*
Belentligi	*plateau*	Hāyk'	*lake, reservoir*	Qulbān	*well-s*
Bi'r	*spring*	Ḥolot	*dunes*	Qurayyāt	*hills*
Birket	*lake, pool, swamp*	Jabal	*hill-s, mountain-s*	Ra's, Râs, Ras	*cape, point*
Boğazı	*strait*	Jazā'ir	*islands*	Ramlat	*dune area*
Buḥayrat	*lake, reservoir*	Jazīrat	*island*	Rhiy	*point*
Burnu, Burun	*cape, point*	Jebel	*hill-s, mountain-s*	Rowd	*river*
Dağ, Dağı	*hill, mountain*	Jībal	*hill-s, mountain-s*	Sabkhat	*salt lake*
Dağları, Dagerşi	*mountains*	Jūn	*bay*	Sha'īb	*ravine, watercourse*
Darya	*river*	Juzur	*islands*	Shatt	*large river*
Daryācheh	*lake*	Kavīr	*salt desert*	Shiqāq, Shiqqat	*elongated depression*
Dasht	*desert*	Kawr	*mountain*	Tall	*hill, mound*
Dawḥat	*bay, cove, inlet, channel*	Khabrat	*depression*	Tepe	*mountain*
Denizi	*sea*	Khalîg, Khalīj	*bay, gulf*	Tur'at	*channel*
'Emeq	*valley*	Khawr	*channel*	Ṭuwayyir	*hill*
Gardaneh	*pass*	Khirbat	*ancient site, ruins*	'Urqūb	*hill, plateau*
Gebel	*mountain-s, range*	Köl	*lake*	'Urūq	*dune area*
Geçidi	*mountain pass*	Körfezi	*bay, gulf*	Wadi, Wādī, Wâdi	*valley, watercourse*
Gezâir	*islands*	Kūh, Kuh	*mountain-s*	Wâḥât'	*oasis*

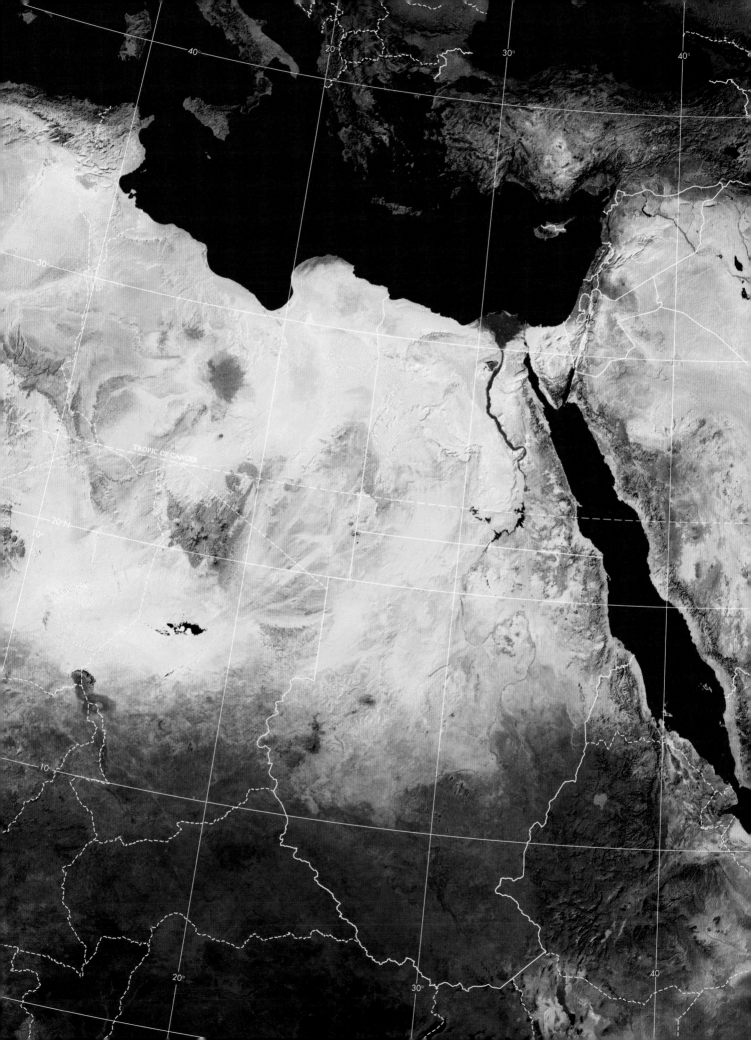

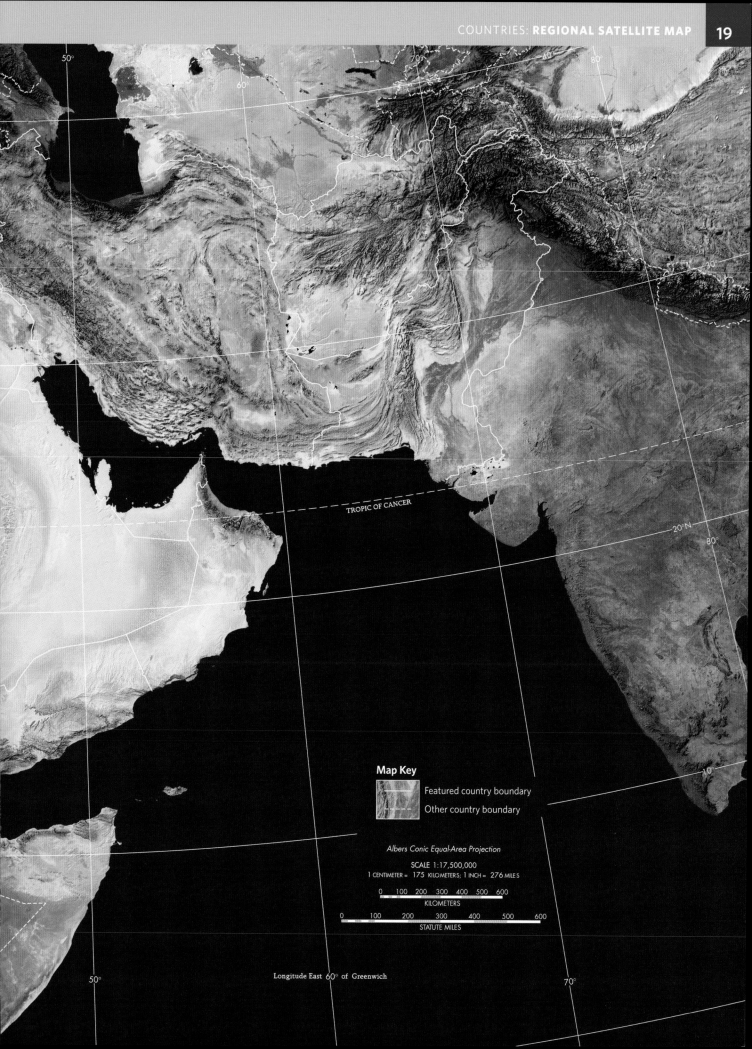

TROPIC OF CANCER

Map Key

Featured country boundary

Other country boundary

Albers Conic Equal-Area Projection

SCALE 1:17,500,000
1 CENTIMETER = 175 KILOMETERS; 1 INCH = 276 MILES

0   100   200   300   400   500   600
KILOMETERS

0   100   200   300   400   500   600
STATUTE MILES

Longitude East 60° of Greenwich

A

QIZILQUM

Fergana Valley

TARIM BASIN

Taklimakan Desert

Garabogaz Bay

Turan Lowland

Qullai Ismoili Somoni (Communism Peak) 7495

Yarkant

KUN

B

4127

CASPIAN SEA

Kuro

G a r a g u m

Amu Darya (Oxus)

Yakhsu

Kongur Shan 7719

K2 (Godwin Austen) 8611

Muztag 6638

LUN MTS.

Absheron Pen. -28

Pamirs

+ 7690

Karakoram Pass 5575

PLATEAU

Aras

4811

Atrak

Köpetdag Mts. 2940

Morghab

Hindu Kush

Nanga Parbat

8126

Karakoram Ra.

OF

Urmia

Eiburz Mountains

2880

Paropamisus Ra.

+ 3494

Khyber Pass 1067

Indus

Ngangiong Range

TIBET

C

Mount Demavend 5671

Dasht-e Kavir

Harirud

Jhelum

Chenab

Ravi

Source of the Indus

Gangdise Range

Namak Lake

2877

Farah

+ 3923

Source of the Ganges

D

Zagros

4548

Dasht-e Lut

2992

Sutlej

Ganges Plain

Shir Küh 4075

Rigestan

3452

Sulaiman Ra.

1046

Yamuna

Ganges

Helmand

3485

Great Indian Desert (Thar Desert)

Banas

Sind

E

Küh-e Hazārān 4420

3188

3280

Küh-e Taftān 4042

Hamun-i-Mashkel

Indus

Luni

Chambal

Parbati

Mountains

Hāmūn-e Jaz Mūriān

Central Makran Ra. 2293

Kech

Vindhya Range

1350

F

Qeshm

Oman Promontory

2087

Sonmiani Bay

Rann of Kutch

Narmada

Satpura Range

Tapi

Hasa Plain

PERSIAN GULF

GULF OF OMAN

TROPIC OF CANCER

Mouths of the Indus

Gulf of Kutch

643

1567

20 N

D A H N A

Sabkhat Matti

1166

Ra's al Hadd

606

Godavari

G

As Sanām

Jabal ash Shām 2980

1433

Umm as Samīm

Masira

DECCAN

Bhima

Manjra

Krishna

Al Hadīdah (meteorite craters)

Gulf of Masira

ARABIAN

PLATEAU

H

RUB AL KHALI (EMPTY QUARTER)

'Urūq Ibn Hamūdah

Ra's ash Sharbatāt

SEA

Penner

Eastern Ghats

J

Manahil

1200

1463

Ghubbat al Qamar

2695

Hadramawt

1730

Ra's Fartak

Map Key

━━━ Featured country boundary

K

Ra's al Kalb

Socotra

──── Other country boundary

Cape Comorin

GULF OF ADEN

'Abd al Kūrī

Cape Gwardafuy

----- Undefined boundary

········ Claimed boundary

··· ··· ··· Disputed boundary

Albers Conic Equal-Area Projection

meters Sea level	feet Sea level
-250	-820
-500	-1,640
-1,000	-3,281
-2,000	-6,562
-3,000	-9,843
-4,000	-13,123
-5,000	-16,404
-6,000	-19,685
-7,000	-22,966

2408

mali Peninsula

SCALE 1:17,500,000

1 CENTIMETER = 175 KILOMETERS; 1 INCH = 276 MILES

0 100 200 300 400 500 600

KILOMETERS

0 100 200 300 400 500 600

STATUTE MILES

INDIAN OCEAN

Depth below sea level

L

M

Longitude East 60° of Greenwich

10 11 12 13 14 15 16 17 18

A
B
C
D
E
F
G
H
J
K
L
M

50°

CASPIAN
Sumqayıt
ERBAIJAN ⊛
BAKI
(Baku)
Stepanakert
(Xankāndi)
Länkäran
Ardabīl
TABRĪZ
Rasht
Zanjān
Qazvīn
ulaymānīyah
andaj Hamadān
QOM
Arāk
Kāshān
Borūjerd
Dezfūl
ESFAHĀN
Yazd
Al 'Amārah
Ahvāz
AL BAŞRAH
Ābādān
Al Kuwayt
(Kuwait)
Al Ahmadī
SHIRĀZ
Bandar-e
Būshehr
KUWAIT
Jahrom
Bandar-e
'Abbās
Ad Dammām
BAHRAIN ⊛ Al Manāmah
AR RIYĀḌ (Manama)
QATAR
(Riyadh) Ad Dawḥah
Abu Dhabi ⊛ (Doha)
D I DUBAI
Al Ḥillah
Matraḥ
'Ibrī
Şūr
UNITED ARAB
EMIRATES
BIA
AR RUB' AL KHĀLĪ
ZUFAR
EMEN
Haḍramawt
Ash Shiḥr
Al Mukallā
OF ADEN
Caluula
LILAND
Garoowe
PUNTLAND
rco (Burao)
Undemarcated
and in Dispute
edweyne
SOMALIA
Gaalkacyo (Galcaio)
Garacad

50°

Reshteh-ye Alborz
(Elburz Mountains)
Kuh-e Zagros
Zagros Mountains
IRAN
KHORĀSĀN

60°

Ţürkmenbaşy
Balkanabat
Aşgabat
(Ashgabat)
Tejen
Mary
Yolöten
Ţürkmenabat
(Chärjew)
Amu Darya
(Oxus)
TURKMENISTAN
Gärabogaz
Aylagy
Daşoguz

Zarafshon
UZBEKISTAN
(Bukhara) Buxoro
Panjakent
Samarqand
Denow
Termiz
TOSHKENT
(Tashkent)
Fergana Valley
KYRGYZSTAN
Dushanbe ⊛
Norak
Kūlob
Khorūgh
TAJIKISTAN

70°

Kashi
(Kashgar)
Shache
(Yarkant)
Hotan

CHINA

80°

Boundary claimed
by India
K2 (Godwin Austen)
8611
AKSAI
CHIN
Boundary claimed
by China
TIBET

Bojnūrd
Quchān
Sabzevār
Neyshābūr
MASHHAD
Torbat-e Heydarīyeh
Herat
(Hirat)
Karokh
Chaghcharan
Birjand
Farah
Zābol
Helmand
Kandahar
Chaman
Zāhedān
Bam
Sīrjān
Rafsanjān
Kermān
BALUCHISTAN
Turbat
Gwadar
Andkhvoy
Mazar-e Sharif
Meymaneh
Baghlan
Bamian
AFGHANISTAN
Ghazni
Qalat
Kondoz
Feyzabad
Hindu Kush
Charikar
KABOL
(Kabul) ⊛
Jalalabad
+7690
+8126
Karakoram Ra.
HIMALAYA
Khorūgh
Mardan
PESHAWAR
Islamabad ⊛
KASHMIR
Srinagar
Jammu
LAHORE
Bannu
Gujranwala
FAISALABAD
Amritsar
Zhob
Sahiwal
Okara
MULTAN
Quetta
Jampur
Bahawalpur
Sibi
Khanpur
Jacobabad
Sukkur
PAKISTAN
Indus
Dadu
Nawabshah
HYDERABAD
Matli
Thatta
KARACHI
Rann of Kutch
LUDHIANA
DELHI
New Delhi ⊛
MEERUT
NEPAL
AGRA
LUCKNOW
KANPUR
Ganges
Bikaner
Alwar
Ajmer
Jodhpur
Kota
Udaipur
INDIA
BHOPAL
AHMADABAD
INDORE
Rajkot
VADODARA
NAGPUR
Jamnagar
SURAT
Nasik
MUMBAI
(Bombay)
KALYAN
PUNE
HYDERABAD
BANGALORE
Mangalore
KOZHIKODE
(Calicut)
KOCHI
(Cochin)
Thiruvananthapuram
(Trivandrum)

PERSIAN
GULF
Str. of Hormuz
Oman
GULF OF OMAN
Masqat
(Muscat)
OMAN
Jazīrat Maşīrah
Salālah

ARABIAN

SEA

TROPIC OF CANCER

20°N

30°

80°

70°

10°

Albers Conic Equal-Area Projection
SCALE 1:17,500,000
1 CENTIMETER = 175 KILOMETERS; 1 INCH = 276 MILES
0 100 200 300 400 500 600
KILOMETERS
0   100   200   300   400   500   600
STATUTE MILES

Suquţrá
(Socotra)
Yemen

MALDIVES
Maale
(Male) ⊛

INDIAN OCEAN

Longitude East 60° of Greenwich

EQUATOR

AFGHANISTAN

Afghanistan

ISLAMIC REPUBLIC OF AFGHANISTAN

Black, the traditional color of Afghanistan, has appeared in all 21 national flags of Afghanistan since recognition of its statehood in 1919. The exception is the plain white flag of the Taliban regime, also often made with the Testimony religious inscription.

AREA	652,090 sq km (251,773 sq mi)
POPULATION	31,890,000
DEMONYM	Afghan(s)
CAPITAL	Kabul 2,994,000
ETHNICITY	

OTHER 4%
BALUCHI 2%
TURKMEN 3%
AIMAK 4%
UZBEK 9%
HAZARA 9%
PASHTUN 42%
TAJIK 27%

RELIGION	Muslim 99% (Sunni 80%, Shiite 19%), other 1%
LANGUAGE	Afghan Persian or Dari (official), Pashtu (official), Turkic languages, 30 minor languages
LITERACY	28.1%
LIFE EXPECTANCY	42 years
TROOPS	Active: 50,000
GDP PER CAPITA	$800
CRUDE OIL RESERVES	None or negligible
ECONOMY	**IND:** textiles, soap, furniture, shoes. **AGR:** opium, wheat, fruits, nuts; wool. **EXP:** opium, fruits and nuts, hand-woven carpets, wool.
AREA COMPARISON	Afghanistan encompasses 8.3% of the 48 contiguous United States; an area slightly smaller than Texas.

AFGHANISTAN

221

BAHRAIN

Bahrain

KINGDOM OF BAHRAIN

When the British suppressed Persian Gulf piracy in the 19th century, Bahrain added a white stripe to its all-red flag, symbolizing peace with Britain. In 2002 Bahrain reduced the stripe zigzags on the flag to five, symbolizing the five obligations of Muslims.

AREA	717 sq km (277 sq mi)
POPULATION	762,000
DEMONYM	Bahraini(s)
CAPITAL	Al Manāmah (Manama) 162,000
ETHNICITY	

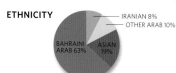

IRANIAN 8%
OTHER ARAB 10%
BAHRAINI ARAB 63%
ASIAN 19%

RELIGION	Muslim 81% (Shiite and Sunni), Christian 9%, other 10%
LANGUAGE	Arabic (official), English, Farsi, Urdu
LITERACY	86.5%
LIFE EXPECTANCY	74 years
TROOPS	Active: 11,200
GDP PER CAPITA	$25,800
CRUDE OIL RESERVES	124,560,000 barrels
ECONOMY	**IND:** petroleum processing and refining, aluminum smelting, iron pelletization, fertilizers. **AGR:** fruit, vegetables; poultry, dairy products; shrimp, fish. **EXP:** petroleum and petroleum products, aluminum, textiles.
AREA COMPARISON	Bahrain encompasses 0.01% of the 48 contiguous United States; an area nearly four times the size of Washington, D.C.

BAHRAIN

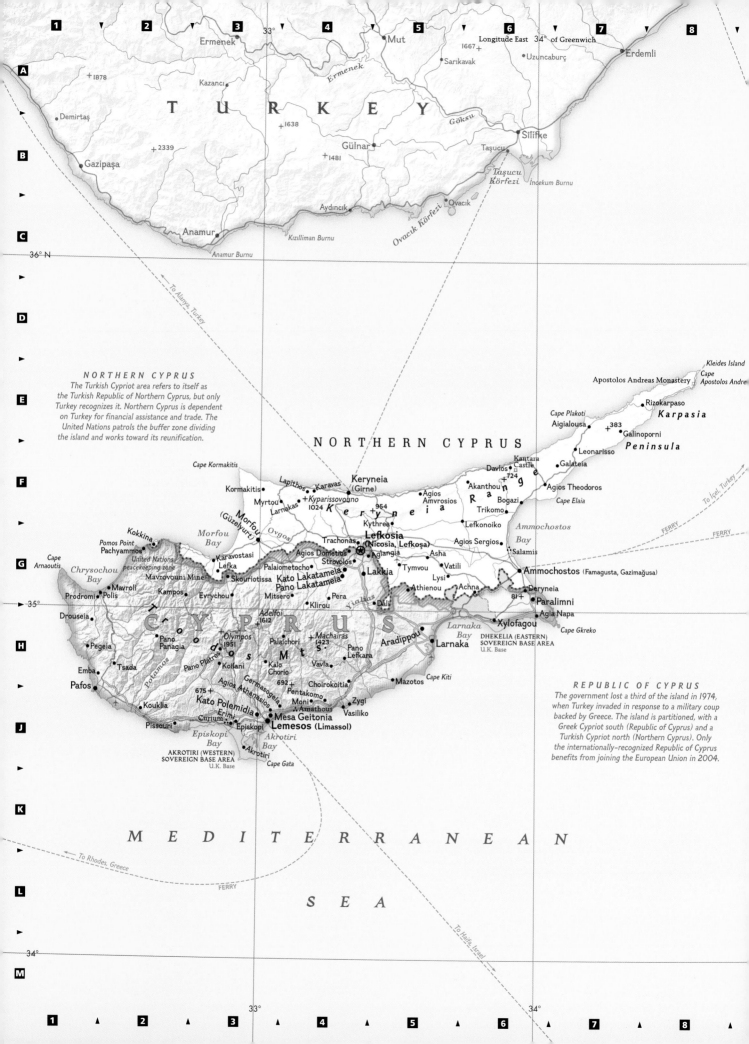

33° 33°

A
+1878

T U R K E Y

• Demirtaş

Ermenek •

Kazancı •

+2339

Mut •

1667 +

Longitude East 34° of Greenwich

Sarıkavak •

Uzuncaburç •

Erdemli •

B

• Gazipaşa

Gülnar •

+1638

+1481

Göksu

Silifke •

Taşucu •

Taşucu Körfezi

İncekum Burnu

C

Anamur •

Aydıncık •

Kızıllıman Burnu

Anamur Burnu

Ovacık •

Ovacık Körfezi

36° N

To Alanya, Turkey

D

E

NORTHERN CYPRUS
The Turkish Cypriot area refers to itself as
the Turkish Republic of Northern Cyprus, but only
Turkey recognizes it. Northern Cyprus is dependent
on Turkey for financial assistance and trade. The
United Nations patrols the buffer zone dividing
the island and works toward its reunification.

Kleides Island

Apostolos Andreas Monastery •

Cape Apostolos Andre

Rizokarpaso •

Cape Plakoti

Aigialousa •

+383

Karpasia

Galinoporni •

Leonarisso •

Peninsula

F

Cape Kormakitis

Lapithos • Karavas •

Keryneia •
(Girne)

Kantara
Castle ▫

Davlos •
+724

Galateia •

N O R T H E R N   C Y P R U S

Kormakitis •

Myrtou •

+Kyparissovouno
1024

Larnakas •

K e r y n e i a

Agios
Amvrosios •

Akanthou •

R a n

Agios Theodoros •

To İçel, Turkey

Morfou
(Güzelyurt)

954 +

Kytkrea •

Trikomo •

Bogazi •

g e

Cape Elaia

FERRY

FERRY

*Morfou
Bay*

Ovgos

Lefkosia •
(Nicosia, Lefkoşa)

Lefkonoiko •

*Ammochostos
Bay*

G

*Cape
Arnaoutis*

Kokkina •

Pomos Point •
Pachyammos •

United Nations
peacekeeping zone

Mavrovouni Mine •

Karavostasi •
Lefka •

Trachonas •

Agios Dometios •
Palaiometocho •
Strovolos •

Aglangia •
Lakkia •

Asha •

Agios Sergios •

Salamis •

Ammochostos • (Famagusta, Gazimağusa)

*Chrysochou
Bay*

Mavroli •

Skouriotissa •

Kato Lakatameia •
Pano Lakatameia •

Tymvou •

Vatili •

Deryneia •

Prodromi • Polis •

Kampos •

Evrychou •

Mitsero •

Pera •

Lysi •

Achna •

81 +

Paralimni •

35°

Drouseia •

Klirou •

Dali •

Athienou •

Yialias

Agia Napa •

H

Pegeia •

*Pano
Panagia*

Adelfoi •
+1612

C Y P R U S

Machairas •
+1423

Aradippou •

*Larnaka
Bay*

Xylofagou •

Cape Gkreko

Emba •

Tsada •

+Olympos
1951

T r o ò d o s   M t s

Palaichori •

Pano
Lefkara •

Larnaka •

DHEKELIA (EASTERN)
SOVEREIGN BASE AREA
U.K. Base

Pafos •

Kouklia •

Potamos

Pano Platres •

Kollani •

Kalo
Chorio •

Vavla •

Choirokoitia •

Mazotos •

Cape Kiti

REPUBLIC OF CYPRUS
The government lost a third of the island in 1974,
when Turkey invaded in response to a military coup
backed by Greece. The island is partitioned, with a
Greek Cypriot south (Republic of Cyprus) and a
Turkish Cypriot north (Northern Cyprus). Only
the internationally-recognized Republic of Cyprus
benefits from joining the European Union in 2004.

Germasogeia •

692 +

Pentakomo •

Zygi •

675 +

Agios Athanasios •

Moni •

Vasiliko •

J

Kato Polemidia •

Amathous •

Erimi •

Curium •

Mesa Geitonia •

Pissouri •

Episkopi •

Lemesos (Limassol)

*Episkopi
Bay*

*Akrotiri
Bay*

Akrotiri •

AKROTIRI (WESTERN)
SOVEREIGN BASE AREA
U.K. Base

Cape Gata

To Rhodes, Greece

K

M E D I T E R R A N E A N

To Haifa, Israel

FERRY

L

S E A

34°

M

33° 34°

CYPRUS

Cyprus

REPUBLIC OF CYPRUS

The flag of Cyprus, created in 1960, symbolizes peace between Greek and Turkish Cypriots. Olive branches frame a silhouette of the island represented in the color of copper, the metal that provided the ancient Greek name for the island.

AREA	9,251 sq km (3,572 sq mi) includes Turkish-occupied region
POPULATION	1,023,000
DEMONYM	Cypriot(s)
CAPITAL	Lefkosia (Nicosia, Lefkoşa) 211,000
ETHNICITY	

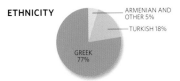

ARMENIAN AND OTHER 5%
TURKISH 18%
GREEK 77%

RELIGION	Greek Orthodox 78%, Muslim 18%, Maronite, Armenian Apostolic, and other 4%
LANGUAGE	Greek (official), Turkish (official), English
LITERACY	97.6%
LIFE EXPECTANCY	78 years
TROOPS	Active: 10,000; Reserves: 60,000
GDP PER CAPITA	Greek Cypriot area: $23,000; Turkish Cypriot area: $7,135
CRUDE OIL RESERVES	None or negligible
ECONOMY	**IND:** tourism, food and beverage processing, cement and gypsum production, ship repair. **AGR:** citrus, vegetables, barley, grapes; poultry. **EXP:** citrus, potatoes, pharmaceuticals, cement.
AREA COMPARISON	Cyprus encompasses 0.12% of the 48 contiguous United States; an area nearly three times the size of Rhode Island.

CYPRUS

Egypt

ARAB REPUBLIC OF EGYPT

In 1958 pan-Arab nationalism inspired the basic Egyptian flag design — stripes of red, white, and black. Two stars symbolized the United Arab Republic, i.e. Egypt and Syria. The current flag, dating from 1984, shows the medieval golden eagle of Saladin.

AREA	1,002,000 sq km (386,874 sq mi)
POPULATION	73,418,000
DEMONYM	Egyptian(s)
CAPITAL	El Qâhira (Cairo) 11,128,000
ETHNICITY	

OTHER 1%
BERBER, NUBIAN, BEDOUIN, AND BEJA 1%
EGYPTIAN 98%

RELIGION	Muslim 90% (mostly Sunni), Christian 10% (Coptic 9%)
LANGUAGE	Arabic (official), English and French widely understood by educated classes
LITERACY	71.4%
LIFE EXPECTANCY	71 years
TROOPS	Active: 468,500; Reserves: 479,000
GDP PER CAPITA	$4,200
CRUDE OIL RESERVES	3,700,000,000 barrels
ECONOMY	**IND:** textiles, food processing, tourism, chemicals, hydrocarbons. **AGR:** cotton, rice, corn, wheat; cattle, water buffalo. **EXP:** crude oil and petroleum products, cotton, textiles, metal products.
AREA COMPARISON	Egypt encompasses 12.8% of the 48 contiguous United States; an area approximately equal to Texas and New Mexico combined.

EGYPT

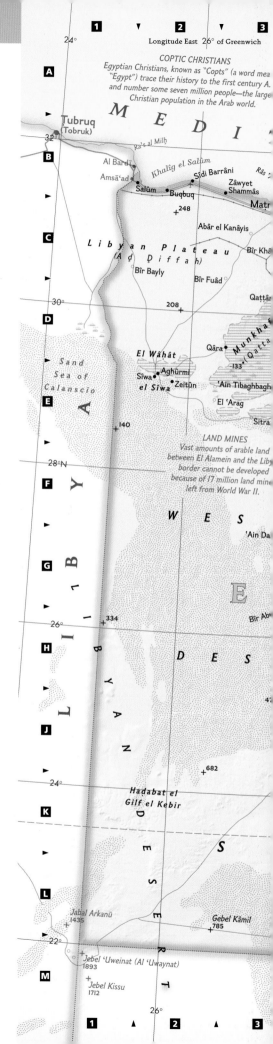

Longitude East 26° of Greenwich

COPTIC CHRISTIANS
Egyptian Christians, known as "Copts" (a word mea "Egypt") trace their history to the first century A. and number some seven million people—the large Christian population in the Arab world.

M E D I

Tubruq (Tobruk)
Ra's al Milḥ
Al Bardī
Khalīg el Salūm
Amsā'ad   Sīdi Barrâni
Salūm   Buqbuq   Zâwyet Shammâs
+ 248
Abâr el Kanâyis   Matr

L i b y a n   P l a t e a u
(A d   Ḍ i f f a h)   Bîr Khā
Bîr Bayly   Bîr Fuâd
Qattâr
208 +

Sand Sea of Calanscio
El Wâhât   Qâra   Munkha (Qatta
-133
Sîwa   Aghûrmi   'Ain Tibaghbagh
el Sîwa   Zeitûn
El 'Arag
Sitra
+ 140

LAND MINES
Vast amounts of arable land between El Alamein and the Lib border cannot be developed because of 17 million land mine left from World War II.

W E S
'Ain Da

E

Bîr Ab
334 +

D E S
+ 682

Hadabat el Gilf el Kebir

S

Jabal Arkanū 1435   Gebel Kâmil 785

Jebel 'Uweinat (Al 'Uwaynat) 1893
Jebel Kissu 1712

26°

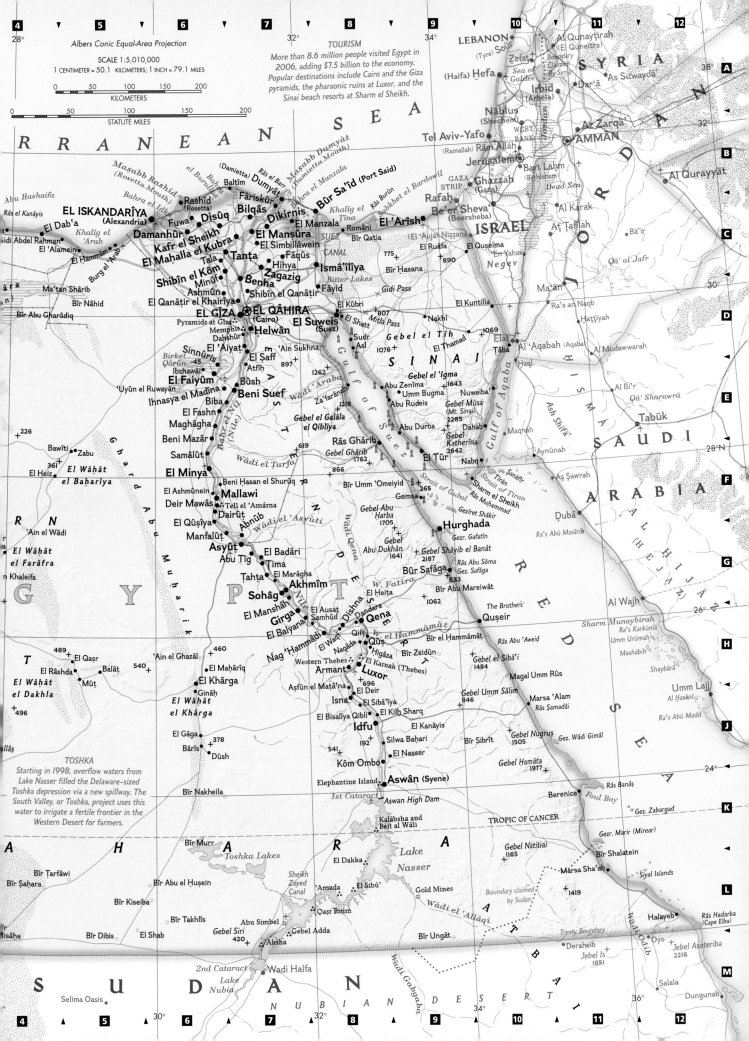

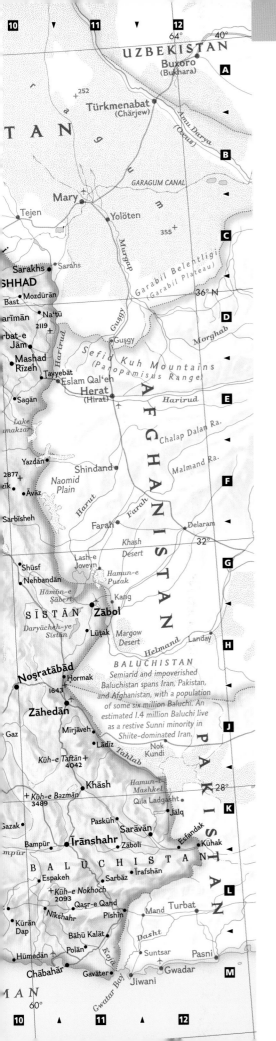

Iran

ISLAMIC REPUBLIC OF IRAN

The 1979 Islamic Revolution modified Iran's green, white, and red flag, adding a new central emblem featuring Muslim symbols. "God Is Almighty" appears on the stripes 22 times, honoring the 22nd of the month of Bahman when the Islamic Revolution was victorious.

AREA	1,648,000 sq km (636,296 sq mi)
POPULATION	71,208,000
DEMONYM	Iranian(s)
CAPITAL	Tehran 7,314,000
ETHNICITY	PERSIAN 51%, AZERI 24%, GILAKI AND MAZANDARANI 8%, KURDISH 7%, ARAB 3%, LUR 2%, BALUCHI 2%, TURKMEN 2%, OTHER 1%
RELIGION	Muslim 98% (Shiite 89%, Sunni 9%), other 2% (Zoroastrian, Jewish, Christian, Baha'i)
LANGUAGE	Persian, Turkic, Kurdish, Luri, Baluchi, Arabic, Turkish
LITERACY	77.0%
LIFE EXPECTANCY	70 years
TROOPS	Active: 545,000; Reserves: 350,000
GDP PER CAPITA	$8,700
CRUDE OIL RESERVES	136,270,000,000 barrels
ECONOMY	**IND:** petroleum, petrochemicals, fertilizers, caustic soda. **AGR:** wheat, rice, sugar beets; dairy products; caviar. **EXP:** petroleum, chemical and petrochemical products, fruits and nuts, carpet.
AREA COMPARISON	Iran encompasses approximately 21% of the 48 contiguous United States.

Iraq

REPUBLIC OF IRAQ

Since independence Iraq's flags have used the four pan-Arab colors. The golden Kurdish sun also appeared briefly. In January 2008, the Iraqi Parliament adopted this new flag for the country retaining the slogan "God Is Almighty" in Kufic script.

AREA	437,072 sq km (168,754 sq mi)
POPULATION	28,993,000
DEMONYM	Iraqi(s)
CAPITAL	Baghdād 5,904,000
ETHNICITY	TURKOMAN, ASSYRIAN, AND OTHER 5% KURDISH 15-20% ARAB 75-80%
RELIGION	Muslim 97% (Shiite 60%-65%, Sunni 32%-37%), Christian and other 3%
LANGUAGE	Arabic (official), Kurdish (official in Kurdish regions), Assyrian, Armenian
LITERACY	74.1%
LIFE EXPECTANCY	57 years
TROOPS	Active: 227,000
GDP PER CAPITA	$2,900
CRUDE OIL RESERVES	115,000,000,000 barrels
ECONOMY	**IND:** petroleum, chemicals, textiles, leather, construction materials. **AGR:** wheat, barley, rice, vegetables; cattle. **EXP:** crude oil, crude materials excluding fuels, food and live animals.
AREA COMPARISON	Iraq encompasses 5.6% of the 48 contiguous United States; an area slightly larger than California.

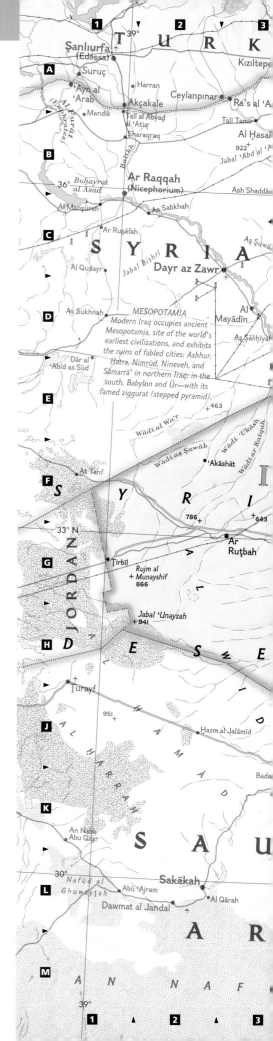

MESOPOTAMIA
Modern Iraq occupies ancient Mesopotamia, site of the world's earliest civilizations, and exhibits the ruins of fabled cities: Ashhur, Hatra, Nimrūd, Nineveh, and Sāmarrā' in northern Iraq; in the south, Babylon and Ūr—with its famed ziggurat (stepped pyramid).

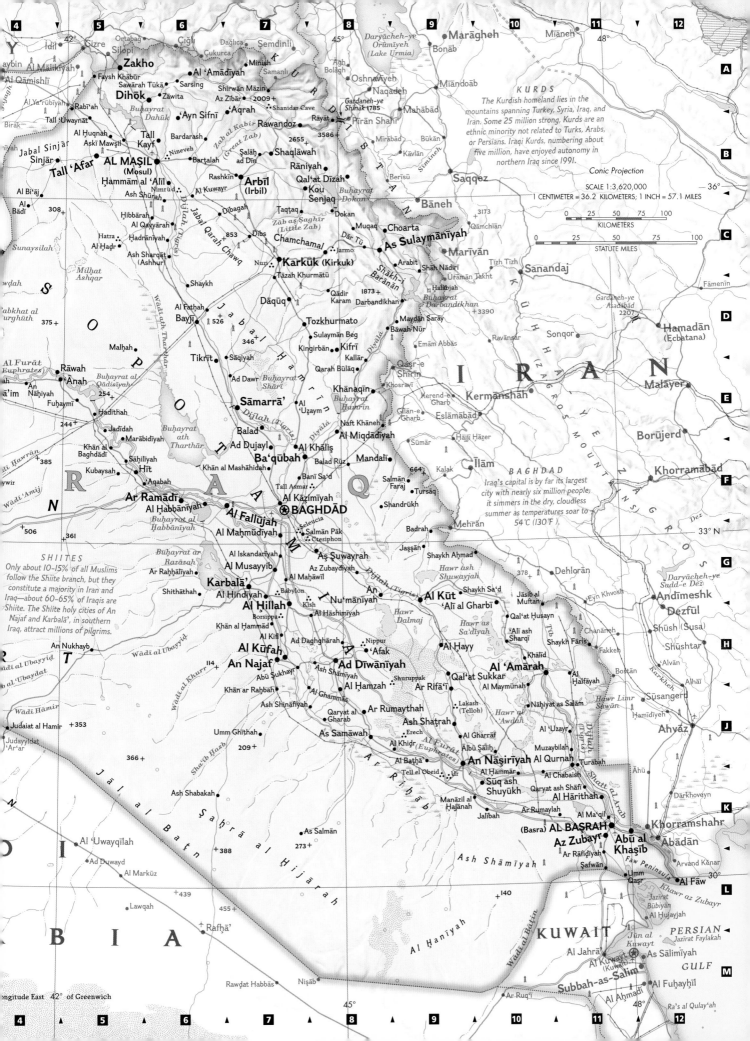

Israel

STATE OF ISRAEL

In 1897 the Zionist Congress (in Basle) authorized a Jewish flag. Its blue stripes recalled the traditional Jewish prayer shawl. The Shield of David for centuries had been associated with Israel. With independence in 1948 the flag was officially recognized.

AREA	22,145 sq km (8,550 sq mi)
POPULATION	7,347,000
DEMONYM	Israeli(s)
CAPITAL	Jerusalem 711,000

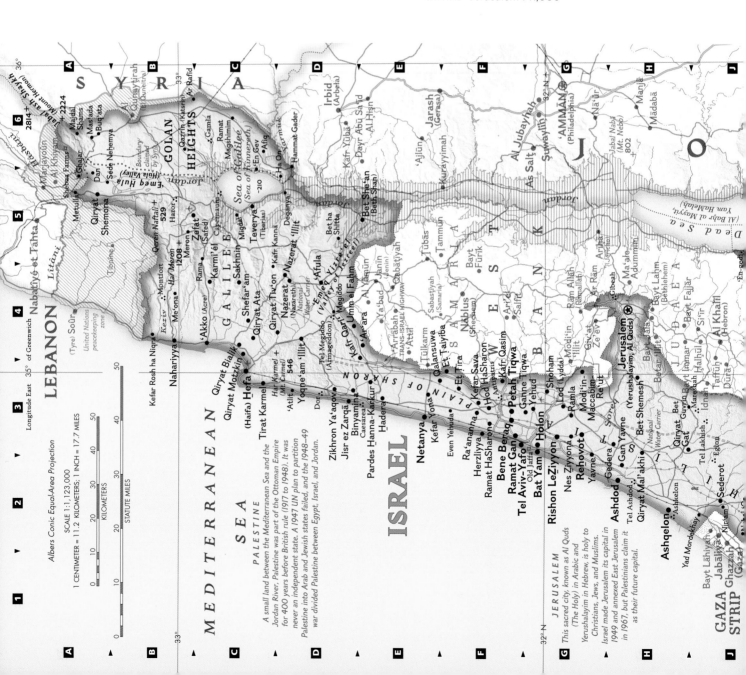

Albers Conic Equal-Area Projection

SCALE 1:1,123,000

1 CENTIMETER = 11.2 KILOMETERS; 1 INCH = 17.7 MILES

PALESTINE
A small land between the Mediterranean Sea and the Jordan River, Palestine was part of the Ottoman Empire for 400 years before British rule (1917 to 1948). It was never an independent state. A 1947 UN plan to partition Palestine into Arab and Jewish states failed, and the 1948–49 war divided Palestine between Egypt, Israel, and Jordan.

JERUSALEM
This sacred city, known as Al Quds (The Holy) in Arabic and Yerushalayim in Hebrew, is holy to Christians, Jews, and Muslims. Israel made Jerusalem its capital in 1949 and annexed East Jerusalem in 1967, but Palestinians claim it as their future capital.

ETHNICITY

OTHER 4.3%
ARAB 19.5%
JEWISH 76.2%

RELIGION   Jewish 76%, Muslim 16%, Christian 2%, other 6%

LANGUAGE   Hebrew (official), Arabic (official for Arab minority), English (commonly used as a foreign language)

LITERACY   97.1%

LIFE EXPECTANCY   80 years

TROOPS   Active: 168,000; Reserves 408,000

GDP PER CAPITA $26,800

CRUDE OIL RESERVES   1,960,000 barrels

ECONOMY   **IND:** high-technology projects (including aviation, communications), wood and paper products, potash and phosphates, food. **AGR:** citrus, vegetables, cotton; beef. **EXP:** machinery and equipment, software, cut diamonds, agricultural products.

AREA COMPARISON   Israel encompasses 0.28% of the 48 contiguous United States; an area approximately the size of Massachusetts.

ISRAEL

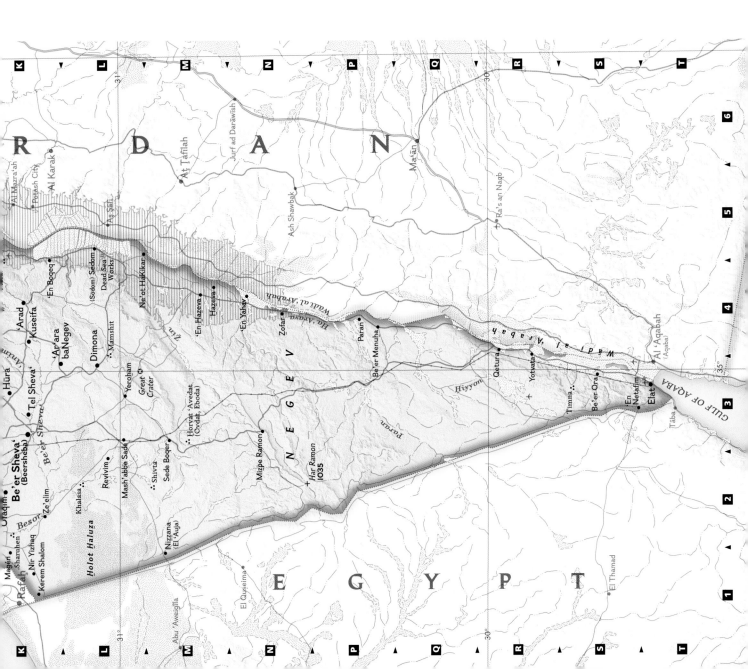

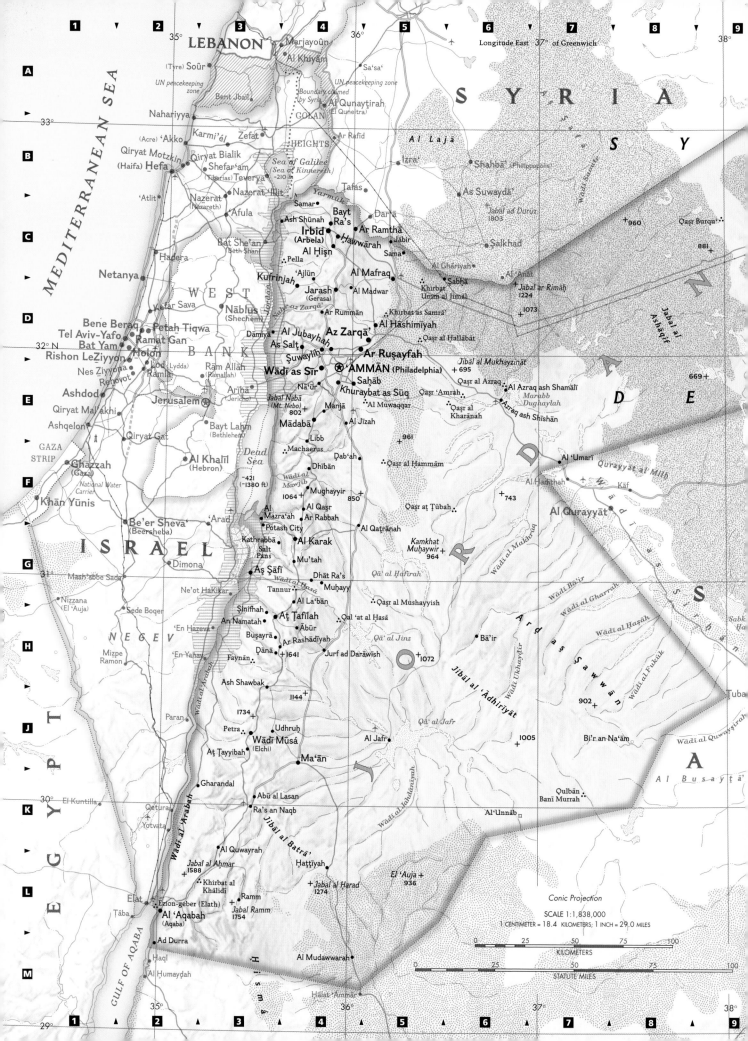

JORDAN

Jordan

HASHEMITE KINGDOM OF JORDAN

In 1917 Arab opponents of Ottoman imperial rule hoisted the Arab Revolt flag. It became the basis for the national flag of Jordan, established in 1921. King Faisal added the star to indicate that he was first among the Arab kings.

AREA	89,342 sq km (34,495 sq mi)
POPULATION	5,728,000
DEMONYM	Jordanian(s)
CAPITAL	'Ammān (Philadelphia) 1,292,000

ETHNICITY

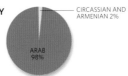

CIRCASSIAN AND ARMENIAN 2%

ARAB 98%

RELIGION	Muslim 94% (Sunni 92%), Christian 6%
LANGUAGE	Arabic (official), English widely understood among upper and middle classes
LITERACY	89.9%
LIFE EXPECTANCY	72 years
TROOPS	Active: 100,500; Reserves: 35,000
GDP PER CAPITA	$5,100
CRUDE OIL RESERVES	1,000,000 barrels
ECONOMY	**IND:** clothing, phosphate mining, pharmaceuticals, petroleum refining. **AGR:** citrus, tomatoes, cucumbers, olives; sheep. **EXP:** clothing, pharmaceuticals, phosphates, fertilizers, potash.
AREA COMPARISON	Jordan encompasses 1.14% of the 48 contiguous United States; an area slightly smaller than Indiana.

JORDAN

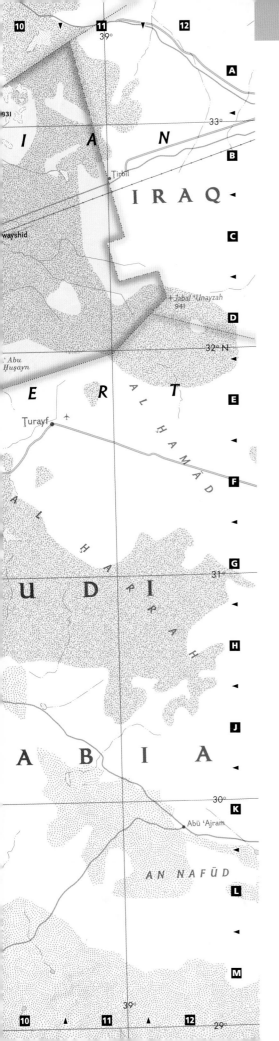

KUWAIT

Kuwait

STATE OF KUWAIT

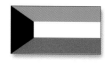

Originally Kuwait, like several other Arab countries, used a plain red flag. In 1917 the country's name was added to the national flag in white. At independence in 1956 a unique new design in the four traditional Arab colors was adopted.

AREA	17,818 sq km (6,880 sq mi)
POPULATION	2,778,000
DEMONYM	Kuwaiti(s)
CAPITAL	Al Kuwayt (Kuwait) 1,810,000
ETHNICITY	

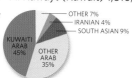

OTHER 7%
IRANIAN 4%
SOUTH ASIAN 9%
KUWAITI ARAB 45%
OTHER ARAB 35%

RELIGION	Muslim 85% (Sunni 60%, Shiite 25%), other 15% (Christian, Hindu, Parsi)
LANGUAGE	Arabic (official), English widely spoken
LITERACY	93.3%
LIFE EXPECTANCY	78 years
TROOPS	Active: 15,500; Reserves: 23,700
GDP PER CAPITA	$23,100 per capita
CRUDE OIL RESERVES	101,500,000,000 barrels
ECONOMY	**IND:** petroleum, petrochemicals, cement, shipbuilding and repair. **AGR:** practically no crops; fish. **EXP:** oil and refined products, fertilizers.
AREA COMPARISON	Kuwait encompasses 0.23% of the 48 contiguous United States; an area slightly smaller than New Jersey.

KUWAIT

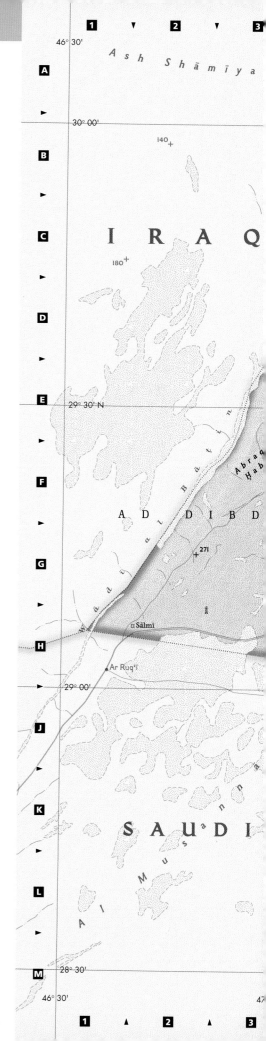

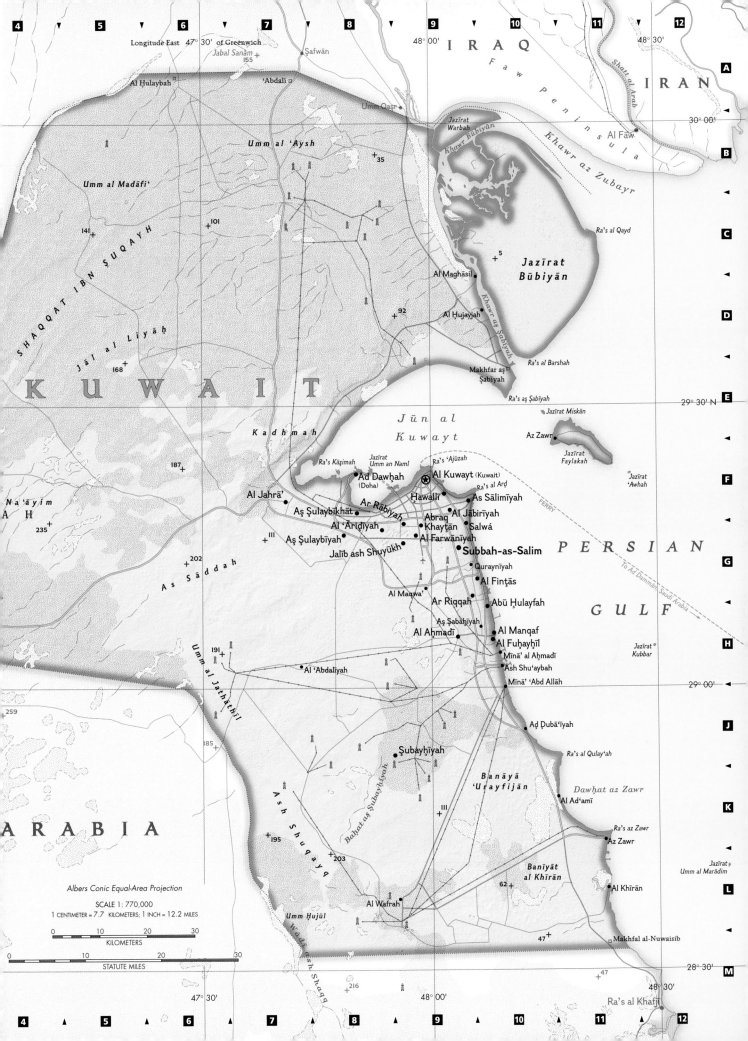

10

Ḥimş (Homs)

A

◄

B

34° 30'

◄

• Ḩisyah

C

◄

D

◄

E

◄

• An Nabk

34° 00'N

F

◄

G

◄

mayr

H

◄

J

33° 30'

◄

K

◄

L

◄

M

LEBANON

Lebanon

LEBANESE REPUBLIC

*During World War II, Lebanon proclaimed independence.
Its new flag, official on November 11, 1943, was based on
one created when Lebanon was a French colony. The cedar
of Lebanon, mentioned in the Bible, was chosen as a
distinctive local symbol.*

AREA	10,452 sq km (4,036 sq mi)
POPULATION	3,921,000
DEMONYM	Lebanese
CAPITAL	Beyrouth (Beirut) 1,777,000
ETHNICITY	

OTHER 1%
ARMENIAN 4%
ARAB 95%

RELIGION	Muslim 60% (Shiite, Sunni, Druze), Christian 39% (Catholic, Orthodox, other), other 1%
LANGUAGE	Arabic (official), French, English, Armenian
LITERACY	87.4%
LIFE EXPECTANCY	71 years
TROOPS	Active: 72,100
GDP PER CAPITA	$5,700
CRUDE OIL RESERVES	None or negligible
ECONOMY	**IND:** banking, tourism, food processing, jewelry. **AGR:** citrus, grapes, tomatoes, apples; sheep. **EXP:** authentic jewelry, inorganic chemicals, miscellaneous consumer goods, fruit.
AREA COMPARISON	Lebanon encompasses 0.13% of the 48 contiguous United States; an area approximately twice the size of Delaware.

LEBANON

OMAN

Oman

SULTANATE OF OMAN

Oman long used a plain red national flag. A new sultan modernized the flag in 1970. It features the red of the old flag, white for religious leaders, and green for the Green Mountain region. The national symbol appears in the upper hoist.

AREA	309,500 sq km (119,499 sq mi)
POPULATION	2,706,000
DEMONYM	Omani(s)
CAPITAL	Masqaṭ (Muscat) 565,000
ETHNICITY	

BALUCHI, EAST AFRICAN, AND OTHER 15.8%
BENGALI 4.4%
OMANI ARAB 48.1%
INDO-PAKISTANI 31.7%

RELIGION	Ibadhi Muslim 75%, other 25% (Sunni Muslim, Shiite Muslim, Hindu)
LANGUAGE	Arabic (official), English, Baluchi, Urdu, Indian dialects
LITERACY	81.4%
LIFE EXPECTANCY	74 years
TROOPS	Active: 41,700
GDP PER CAPITA	$14,400
CRUDE OIL RESERVES	5,500,000,000 barrels
ECONOMY	**IND:** crude oil production and refining, natural and liquefied natural gas (LNG) production, construction, cement. **AGR:** dates, limes, bananas, alfalfa; camels; fish. **EXP:** petroleum, fish, metals.
AREA COMPARISON	Oman encompasses 4% of the 48 contiguous United States; an area approximately the size of New Mexico.

OMAN

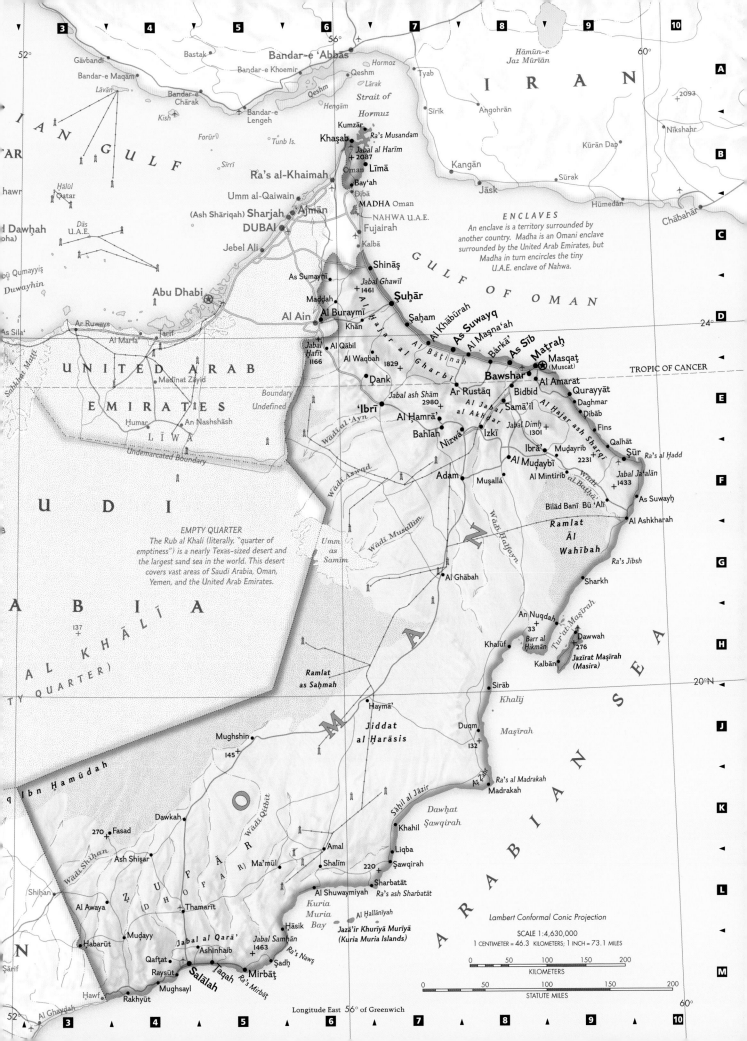

ENCLAVES
An enclave is a territory surrounded by
another country. Madha is an Omani enclave
surrounded by the United Arab Emirates, but
Madha in turn encircles the tiny
U.A.E. enclave of Nahwa.

EMPTY QUARTER
The Rub al Khali (literally, "quarter of
emptiness") is a nearly Texas-sized desert and
the largest sand sea in the world. This desert
covers vast areas of Saudi Arabia, Oman,
Yemen, and the United Arab Emirates.

Lambert Conformal Conic Projection

SCALE 1:4,630,000
1 CENTIMETER = 46.3 KILOMETERS; 1 INCH = 73.1 MILES

KILOMETERS
STATUTE MILES

Longitude East 56° of Greenwich

PAKISTAN

Pakistan

ISLAMIC REPUBLIC OF PAKISTAN

The Muslim League successfully struggled for a separate Islamic Pakistan when India obtained independence in 1947. The Pakistani flag added a white stripe to the League flag (a white crescent on green) for non-Muslims. Today the colors symbolize peace and prosperity.

AREA	796,095 sq km (307,374 sq mi)
POPULATION	169,271,000
DEMONYM	Pakistani(s)
CAPITAL	Islamabad 736,000
ETHNICITY	

OTHER 3.0%
BALUCHI 4.3%
MUHAJIR 7.7%
SINDHI 12.1%
PUNJABI 59.1%
PASHTUN 13.8%

RELIGION	Muslim 97% (Sunni 77%, Shiite 20%), other 3% (Christian, Hindu)
LANGUAGE	Urdu (official), English (official), Punjabi, Pashtu, Sindhi, Siraiki, Baluchi, Hindko, Brahui
LITERACY	49.9%
LIFE EXPECTANCY	62 years
TROOPS	Active: 619,000
GDP PER CAPITA	$2,600
CRUDE OIL RESERVES	289,202,000 barrels
ECONOMY	**IND:** textiles and apparel, food processing, pharmaceuticals, construction materials. **AGR:** cotton, wheat, rice, sugarcane; milk. **EXP:** textiles (garments, bed linen, cotton cloth, yarn), rice, leather goods, sports goods.
AREA COMPARISON	Pakistan encompasses 10.2% of the 48 contiguous United States; an area nearly twice the size of California.

PAKISTAN

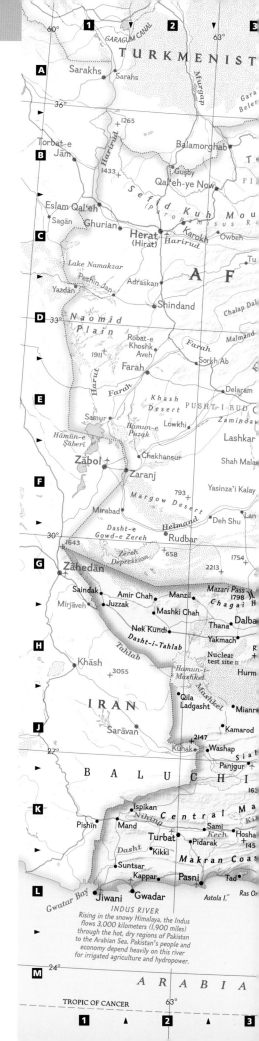

INDUS RIVER
Rising in the snowy Himalaya, the Indus flows 3,000 kilometers (1,900 miles) through the hot, dry regions of Pakistan to the Arabian Sea. Pakistan's people and economy depend heavily on this river for irrigated agriculture and hydropower.

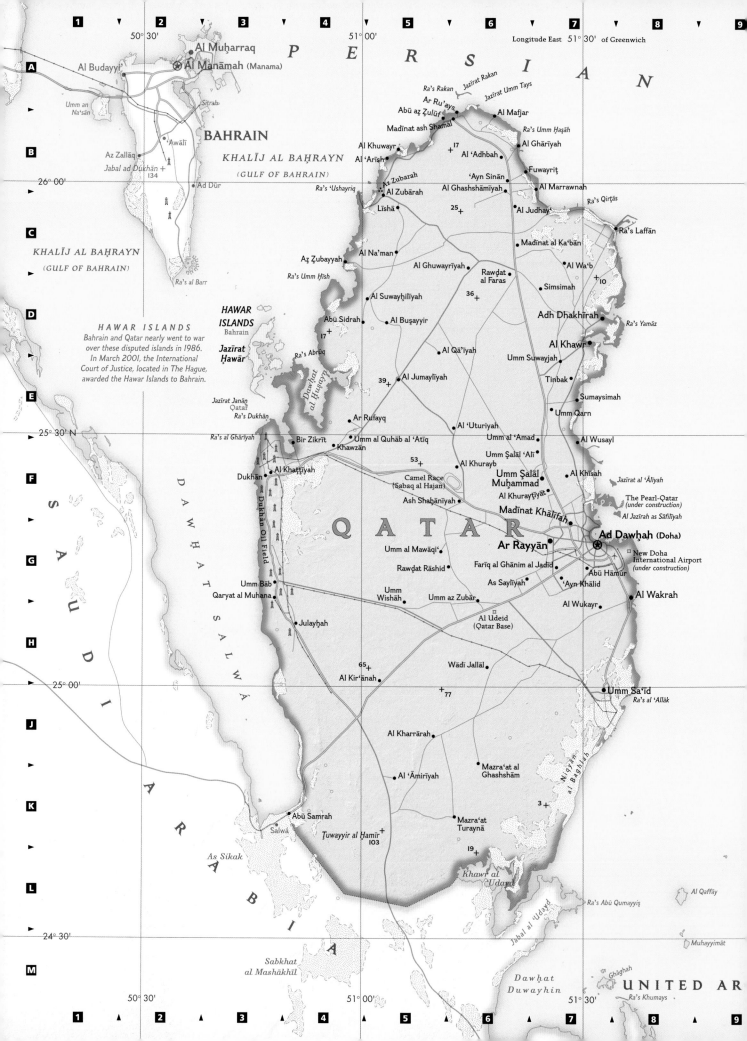

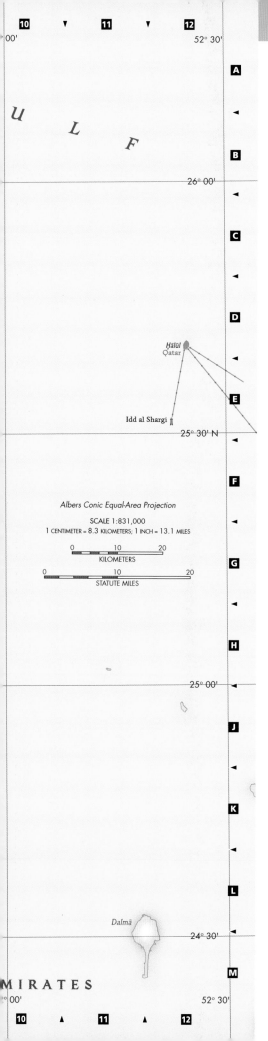

10 00'
11
12 52° 30'

A

B

26° 00'

C

D

Ḥālūl
Qatar

E

Idd al Shargi

25° 30' N

F

Albers Conic Equal-Area Projection

SCALE 1:831,000
1 CENTIMETER = 8.3 KILOMETERS; 1 INCH = 13.1 MILES

0   10   20
KILOMETERS

0   10   20
STATUTE MILES

G

H

25° 00'

J

K

L

Dalmā

24° 30'

M

MIRATES
52° 30'
00'

10
11
12

QATAR

Qatar

STATE OF QATAR

Bahrain long ruled Qatar under its own red and white flag. When the British separated the two countries, the new Qatar flag chosen resembled the old one. However, the zigzags were increased in number and the red stripe was altered to maroon.

AREA	11,521 sq km (4,448 sq mi)
POPULATION	882,000
DEMONYM	Qatari(s)
CAPITAL	Ad Dawḥah (Doha) 357,000

ETHNICITY

ARAB 40%
OTHER 14%
IRANIAN 10%
PAKISTANI 18%
INDIAN 18%

RELIGION	Muslim 78%, Christian 9%, other 13%
LANGUAGE	Arabic (official), English commonly used as a second language
LITERACY	89.0%
LIFE EXPECTANCY	73 years
TROOPS	Active: 12,400
GDP PER CAPITA	$29,800
CRUDE OIL RESERVES	15,207,000,000 barrels
ECONOMY	**IND:** crude oil production and refining, ammonia, fertilizers, petrochemicals. **AGR:** fruits, vegetables; poultry; fish. **EXP:** liquefied natural gas (LNG), petroleum products, fertilizers, steel.
AREA COMPARISON	Qatar encompasses 0.15% of the 48 contiguous United States; an area slightly smaller than Connecticut.

QATAR

SAUDI ARABIA

Saudi Arabia

KINGDOM OF SAUDI ARABIA

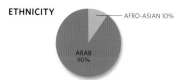

Under a green banner with the Islamic Testimony — There is no god except Allah; Muhammad is the Prophet of Allah — King Abd al-Aziz proclaimed the Kingdom of Saudi Arabia in January 1927. The flag still shows the Testimony and a white sword.

AREA 1,960,582 sq km (756,985 sq mi)

POPULATION 27,601,000

DEMONYM Saudi(s)

CAPITAL Ar Riyāḍ (Riyadh) 4,193,000

ETHNICITY

AFRO-ASIAN 10%

ARAB 90%

RELIGION Muslim 100%

LANGUAGE Arabic (official)

LITERACY 78.8%

LIFE EXPECTANCY 75 years

TROOPS Active: 224,500

GDP PER CAPITA $13,600

CRUDE OIL RESERVES 262,300,000,000 barrels

ECONOMY **IND:** crude oil production, petroleum refining, basic petrochemicals, ammonia. **AGR:** wheat, barley, tomatoes, melons; mutton. **EXP:** petroleum and petroleum products.

AREA COMPARISON Saudi Arabia encompasses 25.1% of the 48 contiguous United States.

SAUDI ARABIA

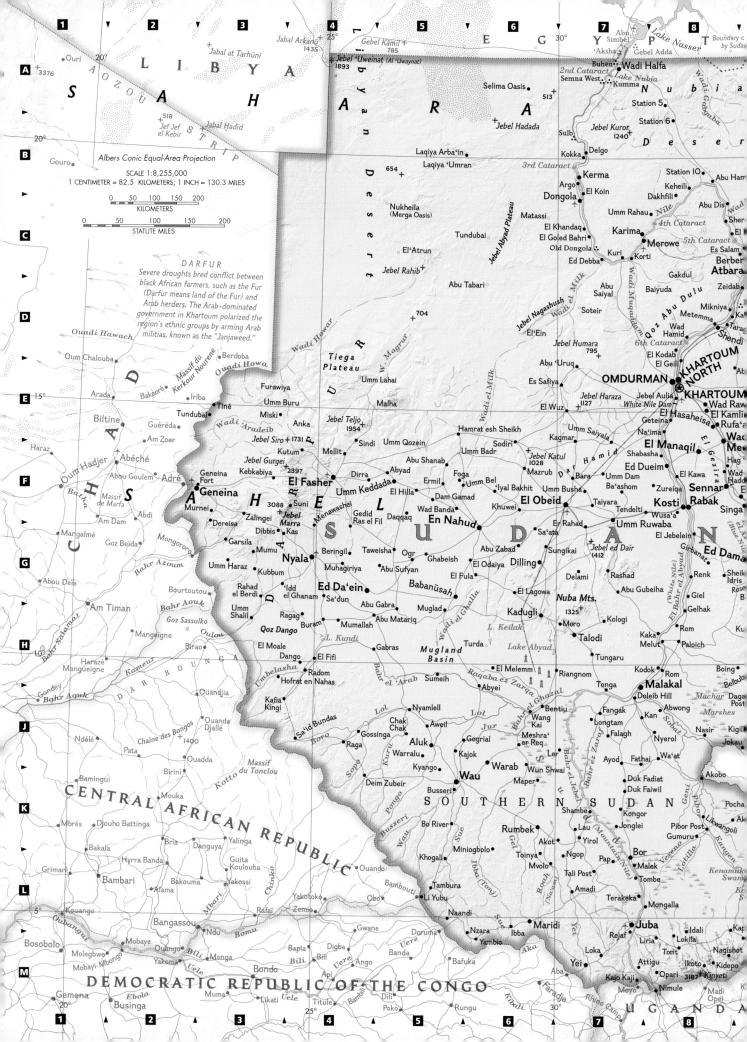

Sudan

REPUBLIC OF THE SUDAN

After long British rule, Sudan became independent in 1956. To emphasize Muslim Arab culture its current flag was adopted in 1970. However, many Christians and animists, hoping for an independent Southern Sudan, already fly its flag which adds yellow and blue.

AREA	2,505,813 sq km (967,500 sq mi)
POPULATION	38,560,000
DEMONYM	Sudanese
CAPITAL	Khartoum 4,518,000

ETHNICITY

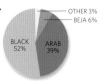

OTHER 3%
BEJA 6%
BLACK 52%
ARAB 39%

RELIGION	Sunni Muslim 70% (in north), indigenous beliefs 25%, Christian 5% (mostly in south and Khartoum)
LANGUAGE	Arabic (official), Nubian, Beja, diverse dialects of Nilotic, Nilo-Hamitic, Sudanic languages, English
LITERACY	61.1%
LIFE EXPECTANCY	58 years
TROOPS	Active: 104,800
GDP PER CAPITA	$2,400
CRUDE OIL RESERVES	5,000,000,000 barrels
ECONOMY	**IND:** oil, cotton ginning, textiles, cement. **AGR:** cotton, groundnuts (peanuts), sorghum, millet; sheep. **EXP:** oil and petroleum products, cotton, sesame, livestock.
AREA COMPARISON	Sudan encompasses 32.0% of the 48 contiguous United States.

SUDAN

Syria

SYRIAN ARAB REPUBLIC

Political changes in Syria since modern statehood in 1919 have resulted in the use of 11 national flags. Almost all featured the four Arab colors. The current design, first used when Syria and Egypt formed the United Arab Republic (1958-1961) was readopted in 1980.

AREA	185,180 sq km (71,498 sq mi)
POPULATION	19,929,000
DEMONYM	Syrian(s)
CAPITAL	Dimashq (Damascus) 2,272,000

ETHNICITY

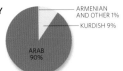

ARMENIAN AND OTHER 1%
KURDISH 9%
ARAB 90%

RELIGION	Muslim 90% (Sunni 74%, Alawite, Druze), Christian 9%, other 1%
LANGUAGE	Arabic (official); Kurdish, Armenian, Aramaic, Circassian widely understood; French, English somewhat understood
LITERACY	79.6%
LIFE EXPECTANCY	73 years
TROOPS	Active: 307,600; Reserves: 354,000
GDP PER CAPITA	$4,100
CRUDE OIL RESERVES	2,500,000,000 barrels
ECONOMY	**IND:** petroleum, textiles, food processing, beverages, tobacco, phosphate rock mining. **AGR:** wheat, barley, cotton, lentils, olives, sugar beets; beef, mutton, eggs, poultry, milk. **EXP:** crude oil, petroleum products, fruits and vegetables, cotton fiber.
AREA COMPARISON	Syria encompasses 2.4% of the 48 contiguous United States; an area approximately the size of North Dakota.

TURKEY

Turkey

REPUBLIC OF TURKEY

Use of the crescent as an Islamic symbol goes back centuries. It was probably introduced by Turkic peoples from central Asia. The red of the modern Turkish national flag is based on what was used by the government during the 19th century.

AREA	779,452 sq km (300,948 sq mi)
POPULATION	73,967,000
DEMONYM	Turk(s)
CAPITAL	Ankara (Angora) 3,573,000

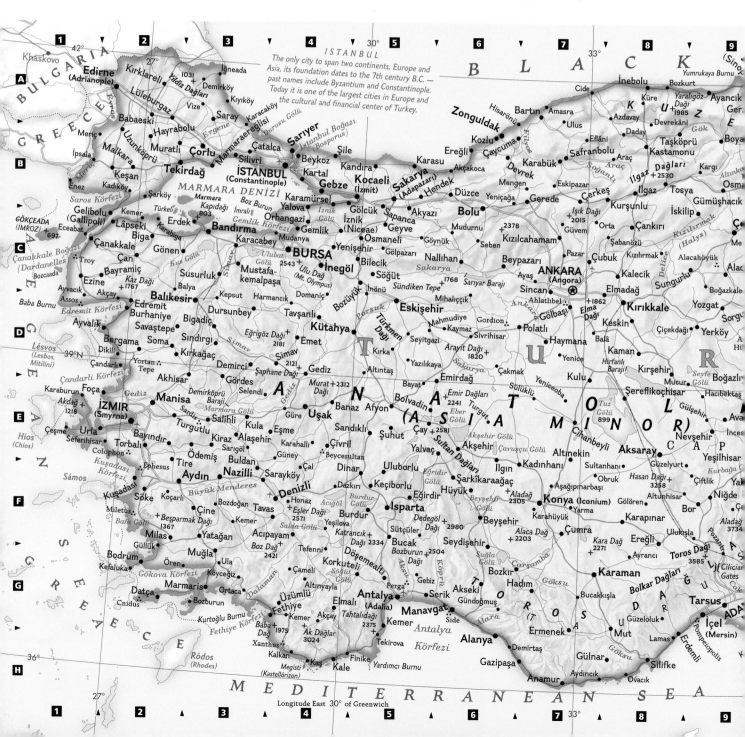

ETHNICITY

KURDISH 20%

TURKISH 80%

RELIGION Muslim 99.8% (mostly Sunni), other 0.2% (mostly Christians and Jews)

LANGUAGE Turkish (official), Kurdish, Dimli (or Zaza), Azeri, Kabardian, Gagauz

LITERACY 87.4%

LIFE EXPECTANCY 72 years

TROOPS Active: 514,850; Reserves: 378,700

GDP PER CAPITA $9,000

CRUDE OIL RESERVES 300,000,000 barrels

ECONOMY **IND:** textiles, food processing, autos, electronics, mining (coal, chromite, copper, boron), steel, petroleum, construction, lumber, paper. **AGR:** tobacco, cotton, grain, olives, sugar beets, pulse, citrus; livestock. **EXP:** apparel, foodstuffs, textiles, metal manufactures, transport equipment.

AREA COMPARISON Turkey encompasses 10.0% of the 48 contiguous United States; an area slightly larger than Texas.

KURDISTAN
Kurds, the largest ethnic minority in Turkey at some 14 million, live in the southeastern highlands — Turkey's poorest region. Clashes between militants of the Kurdistan Workers' Party (PKK) and Turkish armed forces have left villages in ruins and thousands dead.

UNITED ARAB
EMIRATES

United Arab Emirates

UNITED ARAB EMIRATES

Seven Arab states formed the Trucial States Council in 1966. In 1971 the United Arab Emirates became a sovereign nation. Although the flags of all its member states are red and white, the national flag features the four Arab colors.

AREA	77,700 sq km (30,000 sq mi)
POPULATION	4,424,000
DEMONYM	Emirati(s)
CAPITAL	Abu Dhabi 597,000
ETHNICITY	

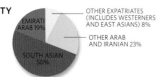

EMIRATI ARAB 19%
OTHER EXPATRIATES (INCLUDES WESTERNERS AND EAST ASIANS) 8%
OTHER ARAB AND IRANIAN 23%
SOUTH ASIAN 50%

RELIGION	Muslim 96% (Shiite 16%); Christian, Hindu, and other 4%.
LANGUAGE	Arabic (official), Persian, English, Hindi, Urdu
LITERACY	77.9%
LIFE EXPECTANCY	79 years
TROOPS	Active: 50,500
GDP PER CAPITA	$49,700
CRUDE OIL RESERVES	97,800,000,000 barrels
ECONOMY	**IND:** petroleum, fishing, petrochemicals, aluminum, cement. **AGR:** dates, vegetables, watermelons; poultry; fish. **EXP:** crude oil, natural gas, dried fish.
AREA COMPARISON	U.A.E. encompasses 0.99% of the 48 contiguous United States; an area approximately the size of South Carolina.

UNITED ARAB
EMIRATES

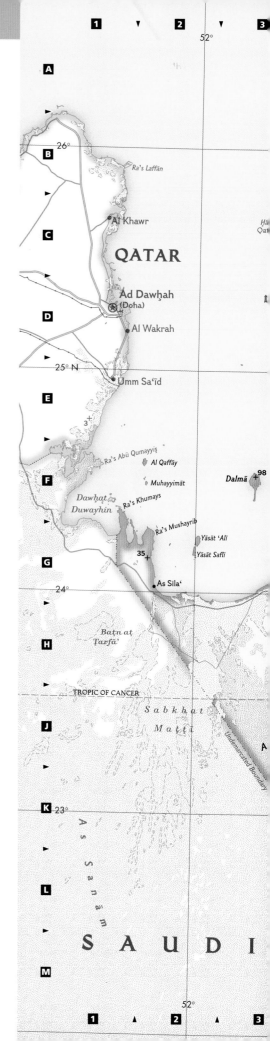

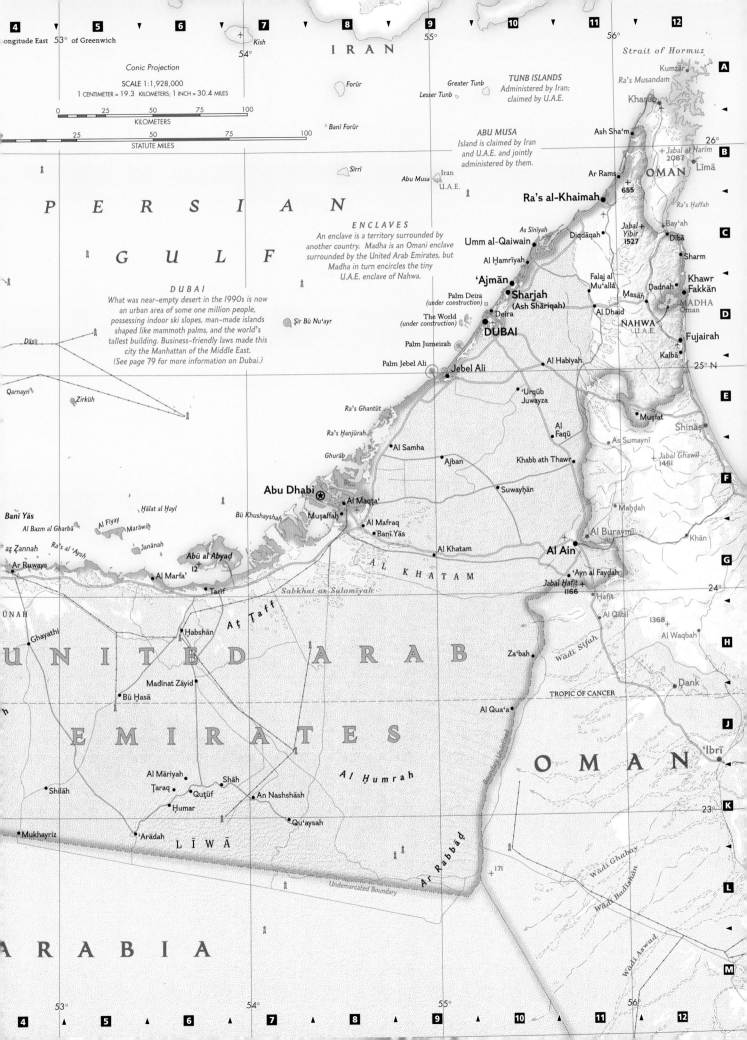

Yemen

REPUBLIC OF YEMEN

It took several decades before the area known as Southern Yemen united with its northern counterpart to form a single country. Their flags were modified to show the features common to the existing flags — horizontal stripes of red, white, and black.

AREA 536,869 sq km (207,286 sq mi)

POPULATION 22,389,000

DEMONYM Yemeni(s)

CAPITAL San'ā' (Sanaa) 1,801,000

YEMEN

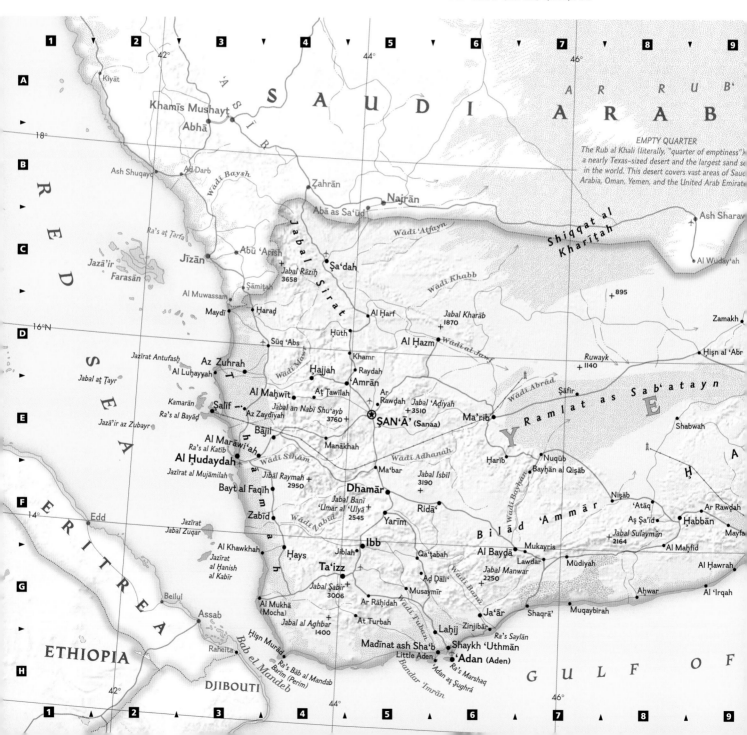

EMPTY QUARTER
The Rub al Khali (literally, "quarter of emptiness") a nearly Texas-sized desert and the largest sand s in the world. This desert covers vast areas of Saud Arabia, Oman, Yemen, and the United Arab Emirate

ETHNICITY

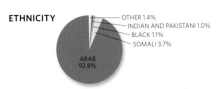

OTHER 1.4%
INDIAN AND PAKISTANI 1.0%
BLACK 1.1%
SOMALI 3.7%
ARAB 92.8%

RELIGION Muslim including Shaf'i (Sunni) and Zaydi (Shiite), small numbers of Jewish, Christian, and Hindu

LANGUAGE Arabic (official)

LITERACY 50.2%

LIFE EXPECTANCY 60 years

TROOPS Active: 66,700

GDP PER CAPITA $1,000

CRUDE OIL RESERVES 3,000,000,000 barrels

ECONOMY **IND:** crude oil production and petroleum refining; small-scale production of cotton textiles and leather goods; food processing. **AGR:** grain, fruits, vegetables, pulses; dairy products; fish. **EXP:** crude oil, coffee, dried and salted fish.

AREA COMPARISON Yemen encompasses 6.9% of the 48 contiguous United States; an area approximately equal to Colorado and Wyoming combined.

YEMEN

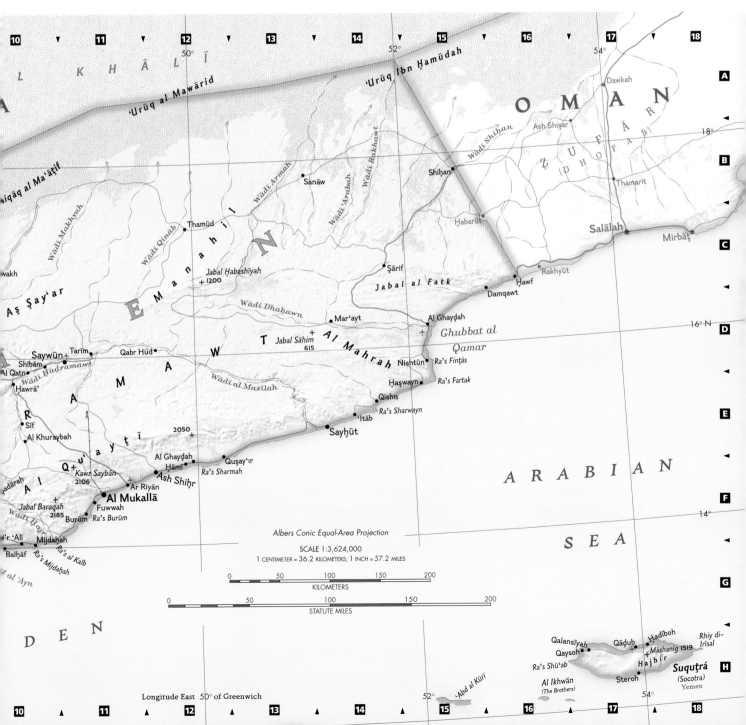

OCCUPIED PALESTINIAN TERRITORIES

Occupied Palestinian Territories

OCCUPIED PALESTINIAN TERRITORIES: WEST BANK AND GAZA STRIP

AREA West Bank: 5,655 sq km (2,183 sq mi); Gaza Strip: 365 sq km (141 sq mi)

POPULATION West Bank: 2,697,000; Gaza Strip: 1,444,000

ETHNICITY West Bank:

JEWISH 17%

PALESTINIAN ARAB AND OTHER 83%

Gaza Strip:

PALESTINIAN ARAB 100%

RELIGION West Bank: Muslim 75% (mostly Sunni), Jewish 17%, Christian and other 8%; Gaza Strip: Muslim 100% (mostly Sunni)

LANGUAGE Arabic, Hebrew (spoken by Israeli settlers and many Palestinians), English (widely understood)

LITERACY 92.4%

LIFE EXPECTANCY 72 years

GDP PER CAPITA West Bank: $1,100; Gaza Strip: $600

CRUDE OIL RESERVES None or negligible

ECONOMY **IND:** generally small family businesses that produce cement, textiles, soap, olive-wood carvings, and mother-of-pearl souvenirs; the Israelis have established some small-scale, modern industries. **AGR:** olives, citrus, vegetables; beef, dairy products. **EXP:** olives, fruit, vegetables, limestone, citrus.

AREA COMPARISON The Occupied Palestinian Territories together encompass 0.08% of the 48 contiguous United States; an area slightly larger than Delaware.

1 **2** **3**
34° 15' 34° 30'

A

Albers Conic Equal-Area Projection
SCALE 1:608,000
1 CENTIMETER = 6.1 KILOMETERS; 1 INCH = 9.6 MILES

0 5 10 15 20
KILOMETERS

0 5 10 15 20
STATUTE MILES

32° 30'

B

△ Palestinian refugee camp
◉/○ Israeli settlement
⌒ Separation barrier, 2007
⌒ Planned barrier

C

32° 15'

D *WEST BANK BARRIER WALL*
Israel began building a separation wall around the West Bank in 2002 to stop Palestinian suicide bombers. The wall often strays from the Israel–West Bank border to include Israeli settlements, considered a violation of international law because it takes occupied land. When completed, the barrier will extend 720 km (450 miles).

E

32° 00'N

F

MEDITERRANEAN SE

G

31° 45'

H *GAZA STRIP*
This sandy strip of land, only 42 km (26 miles) long, was under Egyptian occupation from 1948 until Israel took it in the Six Day War of 1967. In 2005, Israel ended its military rule and evacuated some 8,000 Jewish settlers. Most of the 1.5 million Palestinian inhabitants are refugees, living in overcrowded conditions and dependent on international aid.

Ashqelon
Ashkel
Yad Mordekhay

J

Siafa
Al Qaraya al Badawiya al Maslakh
Bayt Lāhiyah
Bayt Hān
Mukhayyam ash Shati'
Mukhayyam Jabāliyā

Jabāliya

K **GAZA STRIP**
Ghazzah (Gaza)
31° 30'
Al Zahra
(Abu Middein) Al Mughraqa
Mukhayyam Nusayrāt
Juhor ad Dik
Sed
Az Zawayda
Mukhayyam Shaykh al Maghāzī
Mukhayyam al Burayj
Mukhayyam
Dayr al Balah
Dayr al Balah
Wadi as Salqá
Al Má'ani

L
Al Qarara
Grar
Khān Yūnis
Mukhayyam Khān Yūnis
Banī Suhaylah
Abasān al Kabīr
Tal as Sultan
Khuza'a
Al Fuhhārī
Sharuhen
Ofac

M
Rafah
Al Bayuk
Mukhayyam Rafah
31° 15'
Shawkāt aş Şūfī
Gaza International Airport (closed)
Abū 'Awdah
EGYPT 105
34° 15'
34° 30'
Ze'elim

1 **2** **3**

Cities

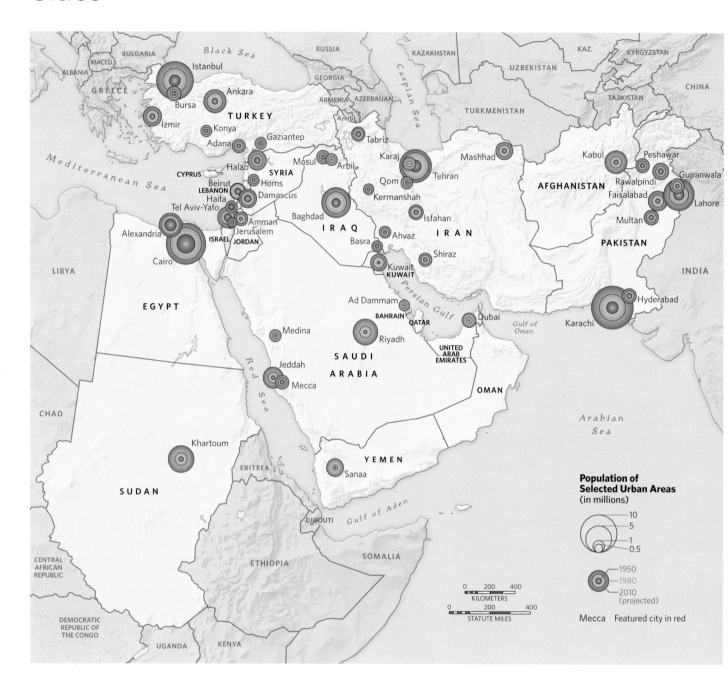

Population of Selected Urban Areas (in millions)

10
5
1
0.5

1950
1980
2010 (projected)

Mecca   Featured city in red

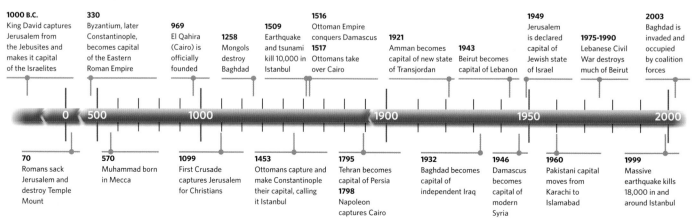

1000 B.C. King David captures Jerusalem from the Jebusites and makes it capital of the Israelites

330 Byzantium, later Constantinople, becomes capital of the Eastern Roman Empire

969 El Qahira (Cairo) is officially founded

1258 Mongols destroy Baghdad

1509 Earthquake and tsunami kill 10,000 in Istanbul

1516 Ottoman Empire conquers Damascus

1517 Ottomans take over Cairo

1921 Amman becomes capital of new state of Transjordan

1943 Beirut becomes capital of Lebanon

1949 Jerusalem is declared capital of Jewish state of Israel

1975-1990 Lebanese Civil War destroys much of Beirut

2003 Baghdad is invaded and occupied by coalition forces

0   500   1000   1900   1950   2000

70 Romans sack Jerusalem and destroy Temple Mount

570 Muhammad born in Mecca

1099 First Crusade captures Jerusalem for Christians

1453 Ottomans capture and make Constantinople their capital, calling it Istanbul

1795 Tehran becomes capital of Persia

1798 Napoleon captures Cairo

1932 Baghdad becomes capital of independent Iraq

1946 Damascus becomes capital of modern Syria

1960 Pakistani capital moves from Karachi to Islamabad

1999 Massive earthquake kills 18,000 in and around Istanbul

Key to City Maps

• Populated place   ⎯⎯ Super highway   ⎯⎯ Other road   ‑‑‑‑ Railroad   ⎯⎯ Perennial drainage   ▢ Built-up area
□ Point of interest   ⎯⎯ Highway   ⎯⎯ Tunnel   ‑‑‑‑ Administrative boundary   ‑‑‑ Intermittent drainage

Dashed lines represent roads under construction.

Amman, Jordan

AT A GLANCE

POPULATION	1,292,000
CITY ELEVATION	785 meters 2,575 feet
LATITUDE	31° 57' N
LONGITUDE	35° 56' E
TEMPERATURE Average Daily High/Low	Jan. 54°/38°F (12°/4°C) July 90°/65°F (32°/19°C)
RAINFALL Average Monthly inches	Jan. 2.5 July 0.0
TIME ZONE	+2 hours UTC

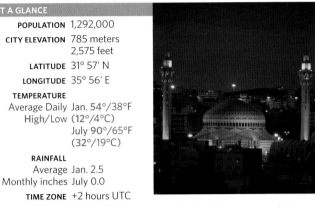

MAJOR INDUSTRIES: Food and tobacco processing, textiles, paper products, plastics, aluminum utensils.

Once the capital of the Ammonites, Amman later survived under the control of the Assyrians, then the Persians, followed by the Greeks (who called it Philadelphia), and then the Romans. The city then languished for hundreds of years, returning to prominence after World War I. Jordan's capital has experienced several different population booms related to floods of refugees, most notably in 1948 and 1967 after Arab-Israeli wars. Clashes between the Jordanian Army and Palestinian guerillas in 1970 destroyed large parts of city, which has recently undergone another population boom fueled by refugees—this time from Iraq.

Baghdad, Iraq

AT A GLANCE

POPULATION	5,904,000
CITY ELEVATION	34 meters 112 feet
LATITUDE	33° 21' N
LONGITUDE	44° 25' E
TEMPERATURE Average Daily High/Low	Jan. 61°/39°F (16°/4°C) July 109°/75°F (43°/24°C)
RAINFALL Average Monthly inches	Jan. 1.1 July 0.0
TIME ZONE	+3 hours UTC

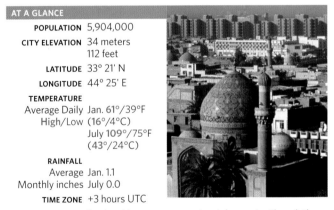

MAJOR INDUSTRIES: Food and beverage processing, tobacco, textiles, clothes, leather goods, wood products, furniture, paper and printed material, bricks.

Relatively young as Middle Eastern cities go, Baghdad was founded in 762 by Mansur, caliph of the Abbasid dynasty. It soon rose to become one of the most important cities of Islam and a center of Arabic scholarship and arts. Rapidly modernized during the early 1980s, Iraq's capital was heavily bombed during the 1991 Gulf War. Since the 2003 invasion of Iraq and the ousting of Saddam Hussein's regime, Baghdad has endured an evolving state of unrest. Escalating sectarian violence led to much of the city being divided into Shiite and Sunni halves, while most parts of the city have suffered from a lack of security and vital services like electricity.

Beirut, Lebanon

POPULATION	1,777,000
CITY ELEVATION	24 meters
	79 feet
LATITUDE	33° 53' N
LONGITUDE	35° 30' E
TEMPERATURE	
Average Daily	Jan. **63°/52°F**
High/Low	(**17°/11°C**)
	July **88°/73°F**
	(**31/23°C**)
RAINFALL	
Average	Jan. 7.4
Monthly inches	July 0.0
TIME ZONE	+2 hours UTC

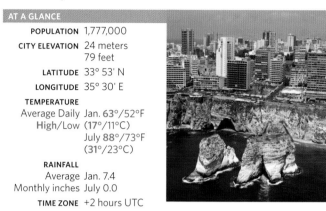

MAJOR INDUSTRIES: Printing, small-scale and home-based industries.

Beirut

Massively ravaged during the 1975-1990 civil war, which split the city along the infamous Green Line dividing its Muslim west from its Christian east, Lebanon's capital has been extensively rebuilt. Billions of dollars in renovations transformed the ruined "Paris of the Middle East" into a fair reflection of what it was before the civil war: a capital of fashion, banking, trade, international conferences, nightlife, and tourism. In the 2006 conflict between Israel and Lebanon, Beirut sustained significant damage from Israeli air strikes targeting Hezbollah's infrastructure. Hezbollah, with financial backing from Iran, worked quickly to rebuild these areas.

Cairo, Egypt

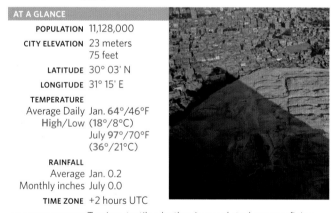

POPULATION	11,128,000
CITY ELEVATION	23 meters
	75 feet
LATITUDE	30° 03' N
LONGITUDE	31° 15' E
TEMPERATURE	
Average Daily	Jan. **64°/46°F**
High/Low	(**18°/8°C**)
	July **97°/70°F**
	(**36°/21°C**)
RAINFALL	
Average	Jan. 0.2
Monthly inches	July 0.0
TIME ZONE	+2 hours UTC

MAJOR INDUSTRIES: Tourism, textiles, leather, iron and steel, sugar refining, food and tobacco processing.

Cairo

Cairo, one of the Middle East's largest cities with more than eleven million people, straddles the Nile just south of the river's great delta. El Qahira (Cairo), which means "The Triumphant" in Arabic, became the Egyptian capital after the previous capital, Fustat, was destroyed in 1168 in order to foil a Crusader army. Ancient Egyptian, Roman, Arabic, and Turkish monuments proclaim vital links with history; today Cairo's rich contrasts, ancient pyramids, modern skyscrapers, fragrant bazaars, towering palm trees, industry and commerce, suburbs and shantytowns, mosques and minarets, make it a center of Arab culture.

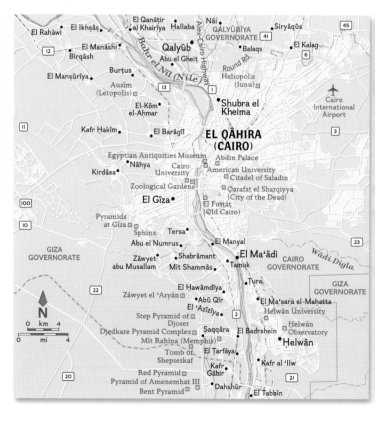

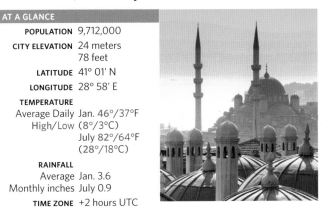

Damascus, Syria

AT A GLANCE	
POPULATION	2,272,000
CITY ELEVATION	707 meters
	2,320 feet
LATITUDE	33° 30' N
LONGITUDE	36° 18' E
TEMPERATURE	
Average Daily	Jan. 54°/36°F
High/Low	(12°/2°C)
	July 97°/64°F
	(36°/18°C)
RAINFALL	
Average	Jan. 1.5
Monthly inches	July 0.0
TIME ZONE	+2 hours UTC

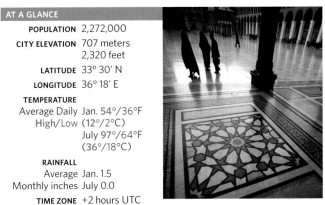

MAJOR INDUSTRIES: Damask fabric, metalware, leather goods, refined sugar, chemicals, cement.

Damascus

Built on a desert oasis nourished by the Barada River, Syria's capital is among the world's oldest continuously inhabited cities. Conquering armies, kingdoms, dynasties, and empires have swept through for thousands of years, but Damascus has been spared from extensive damage in modern conflicts. Sometimes called "The Pearl of the East," the city remains famous for its ancient markets, museums, remnants of Roman walls, and the eighth-century Umayyad Mosque, considered one of the world's finest examples of Islamic architecture. Damascus is also a historical origin point for the Islamic pilgrimage road (the Darb al-Hajj) leading to Mecca.

Istanbul, Turkey

AT A GLANCE	
POPULATION	9,712,000
CITY ELEVATION	24 meters
	78 feet
LATITUDE	41° 01' N
LONGITUDE	28° 58' E
TEMPERATURE	
Average Daily	Jan. 46°/37°F
High/Low	(8°/3°C)
	July 82°/64°F
	(28°/18°C)
RAINFALL	
Average	Jan. 3.6
Monthly inches	July 0.9
TIME ZONE	+2 hours UTC

MAJOR INDUSTRIES: Shipbuilding, cement, textiles, glass, pottery, leather goods, flour milling, tobacco processing, tourism.

Istanbul

Founded by Greeks as Byzantium around 660 B.C., this city on a thumb of land along the Bosporus would become one of the most influential cities of all time. The city eventually held the seat of the Roman Empire in 330 and became known as Constantinople. Its location has been strategically vital to world trade and power for millennia, being situated on a major route between Europe and Asia. The Turkish government officially renamed the city Istanbul in 1930, and the uniquely cosmopolitan city has since expanded to straddle the narrow gap between the two continents.

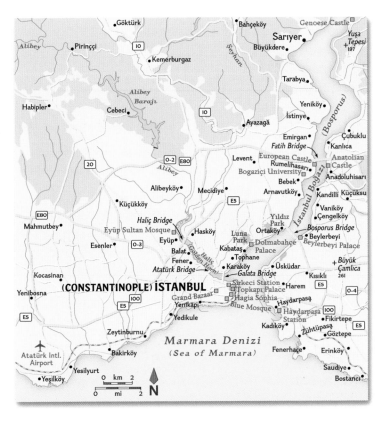

Jerusalem, Israel

POPULATION	711,000
CITY ELEVATION	800 meters 2,625 feet
LATITUDE	31° 47' N
LONGITUDE	35° 14' E
TEMPERATURE Average Daily High/Low	Jan. 55°/41°F (13°/5°C) July 88°/63°F (31°/17°C)
RAINFALL Average Monthly inches	Jan. 5.5 July 0.0
TIME ZONE	+2 hours UTC

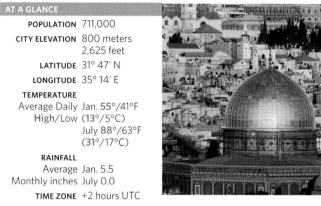

MAJOR INDUSTRIES: Tourism, diamond-cutting, electronic equipment, wood, furniture, paper and printing, textiles, service-based industries.

Jerusalem

Medieval cartographers located Jerusalem at the center of the world, and in the eyes of many the Old City remains so. For Jews, the Western Wall of the Second Temple is the holiest of sites. Above it is the Dome of the Rock, third holiest site in Islam, commemorating the place where Muhammad ascended to heaven. A few blocks away the Church of the Holy Sepulchre marks the traditional site where Jesus was crucified, entombed, and resurrected. Israel claims the city as its eternal capital; Palestinians assert that East Jerusalem should be the capital of their independent state.

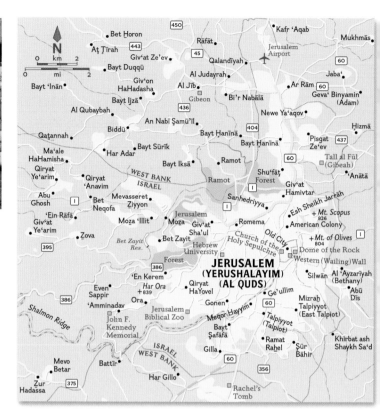

Karachi, Pakistan

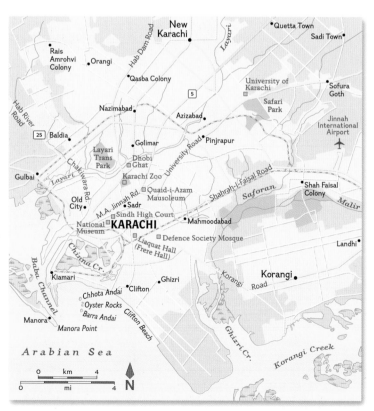

POPULATION	11,608,000
CITY ELEVATION	15 meters 49 feet
LATITUDE	24° 52' N
LONGITUDE	67° 03' E
TEMPERATURE Average Daily High/Low	Jan. 77°/55°F (25°/13°C) July 91°/81°F (33°/27°C)
RAINFALL Average Monthly inches	Jan. 0.3 July 3.5
TIME ZONE	+5 hours UTC

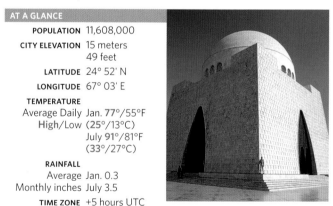

MAJOR INDUSTRIES: Textiles, footwear, steel, engineering, oil refining, motor vehicles, food and beverages, paper and printing, chemicals, petroleum.

Karachi

The mausoleum of Muhammad Ali Jinnah, principal founder of modern Pakistan, stands in calm contrast to teeming Karachi. Once the capital and still the nation's largest city, the former fishing village has absorbed Muslim immigrants from around the region—from India (most notably after the 1947 partition of the British Indian Empire into Hindu and Muslim states), Afghanistan, and from other regions of Pakistan. Some 300,000 arrive yearly to an already crowded city swept by ethnic feuds, corruption, and occasional terrorist acts. Still, the city of over 11 million remains important as a center for culture, commerce, and transportation.

Mecca, Saudi Arabia

AT A GLANCE

POPULATION 1,319,000

CITY ELEVATION 291 meters
955 feet

LATITUDE 21° 26' N

LONGITUDE 39° 50' E

TEMPERATURE
Average Daily Jan. 86°/66°F
High/Low (30°/19°C)
July 109°/84°F
(43°/29°C)

RAINFALL
Average Jan. 0.6
Monthly inches July 0.1

TIME ZONE +3 hours UTC

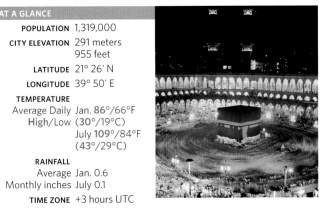

MAJOR INDUSTRIES: Textiles, furniture, utensils, service-based industries.

Birthplace (in the year 570) of the Prophet Muhammad, Mecca is the most sacred city in Islam. In Mecca's Sacred Mosque is the Kaaba, Islam's holiest place, toward which all Muslims direct their regular prayers—and around which millions of pilgrims circumambulate while performing the annual Hajj pilgrimage. The city has grown in modern times to over a million people, as travel to Mecca has become easier and demand for services from pilgrims has exploded. Very little industry bolsters the city's economy, which is sustained by subsidies and the money generated by pilgrimages. Non-Muslims are not permitted to enter the city.

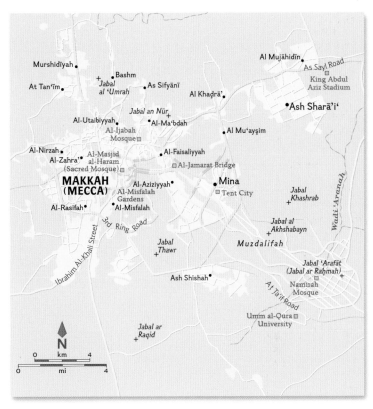

Tehran, Iran

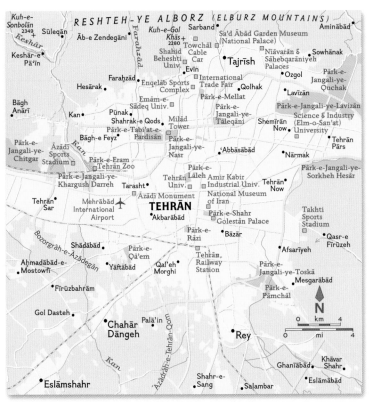

AT A GLANCE

POPULATION 7,314,000

CITY ELEVATION 1,139 meters
3,736 feet

LATITUDE 35° 40' N

LONGITUDE 51° 26' E

TEMPERATURE
Average Daily Jan. 45°/27°F
High/Low (7°/-3°C)
July 99°/72°F
(37°/22°C)

RAINFALL
Average Jan. 1.7
Monthly inches July 0.1

TIME ZONE +3.5 hours UTC

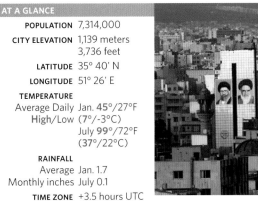

MAJOR INDUSTRIES: Textiles, cement, sugar, pottery, electrical equipment, pharmaceuticals.

Iran's Elburz Mountains overlook the high, expansive capital of Tehran (3,736 feet). Fittingly, Tehran translates as "at the bottom of the mountain" in Persian. The city's Muslim population, a multi-ethnic mix of majority Persians, Azeris, Kurds, Arabs, and tribal groups, grew rapidly in the 1980s; rising birthrates, rural to urban migration, and refugees from Afghanistan and war with Iraq swelled the city. Religious minorities—Armenian and Assyrian Christians, Zoroastrians, and Jews—have lived here for centuries. Iran's Pahlavi dynasty, founded in 1925, ended in 1979 with the establishment of an Islamic Republic under Ayatollah Khomeini.

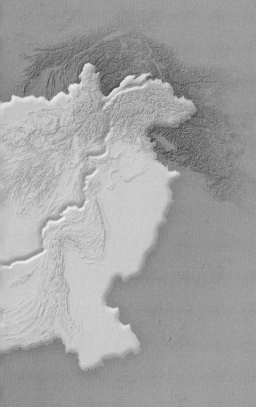

Regional Themes

Climate

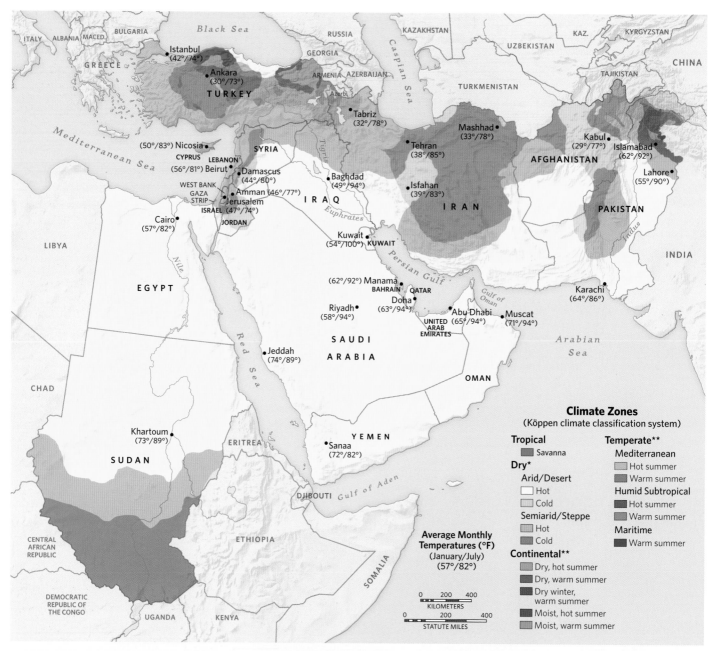

TROPICAL: SAVANNA
Characterized by drought-resistant grasslands and scattered trees, savannas are seen as a transitional zone between rain forests and deserts. Rain fluctuates greatly throughout the year with a distinct warm, wet season and a hot, dry season.

DRY: ARID/DESERT
Fifty percent of the Middle East is classified as arid/desert. This climate type is typically the result of a persistent high-pressure area, and is characterized by sparse vegetation, negligible annual rainfall, and some seasonal variation in temperature.

DRY: SEMIARID/STEPPE
This climate type is often found in inland regions, in the rain shadow of mountain ranges. The monthly temperatures cover a much greater range and the areas receive significantly more rain than do deserts. Annual rainfall amounts support mainly grasses and small shrubs. Twenty percent of the Middle East has this climate type.

CONTINENTAL
These areas are marked by temperature extremes, as large variations can be found between monthly temperatures. Rainfall ranges from moderate to abundant. In the Middle East, this climate is found in northern Pakistan and northeastern Turkey.

TEMPERATE: MEDITERRANEAN
This term describes much of the Mediterranean region. In the Middle East, it is also found in areas east of the Tigris River and along the Caspian and Black Seas. Summer months are typically warm to hot with dry conditions, while winters are cool and provide modest precipitation. Thirty percent of the Middle East falls into this category.

TEMPERATE: HUMID SUBTROPICAL
Found in northern Pakistan, warm, humid summers and winters that bring cold snaps and snowy periods characterize this climate zone.

TEMPERATE: MARITIME
Prevailing westerly winds bring mild ocean air ashore, but sunny days are limited and precipitation is frequent. Except in the highest elevations, most precipitation falls as rain. This climate supports extensive forests.

*Arid/Desert and Semiarid/Steppe
HOT: Mean annual temperature greater than or equal to 64°F (18°C)

COLD: Mean annual temperature is less than 64° F (18°C)

**Temperate and Continental
HOT SUMMER: Temperature in the warmest month is greater than or equal to 72°F (22°C)

WARM SUMMER: Temperature in the warmest month is less than 72° F (22°C), and four or more months with a temperature greater than or equal to 50° F (10°C)

MEAN JANUARY TEMPERATURE

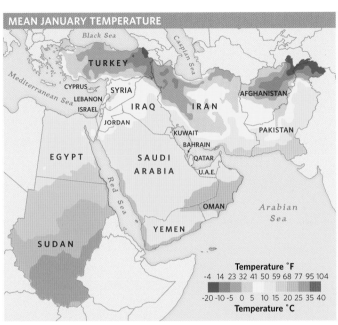

Temperature °F
-4 14 23 32 41 50 59 68 77 95 104

-20 -10 -5 0 5 10 15 20 25 35 40
Temperature °C

MEAN JANUARY PRECIPITATION

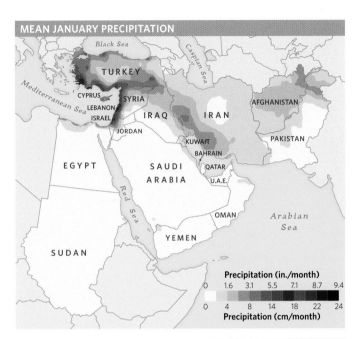

Precipitation (in./month)
0 1.6 3.1 5.5 7.1 8.7 9.4

0 4 8 14 18 22 24
Precipitation (cm/month)

MEAN JULY TEMPERATURE

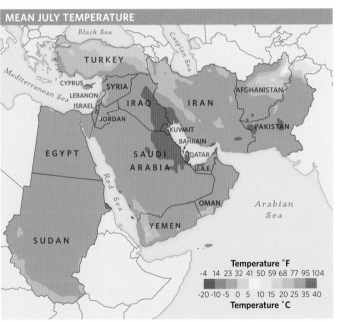

Temperature °F
-4 14 23 32 41 50 59 68 77 95 104

-20 -10 -5 0 5 10 15 20 25 35 40
Temperature °C

MEAN JULY PRECIPITATION

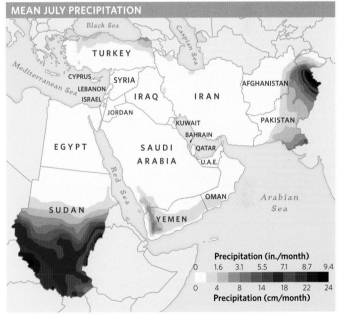

Precipitation (in./month)
0 1.6 3.1 5.5 7.1 8.7 9.4

0 4 8 14 18 22 24
Precipitation (cm/month)

MEAN MONTHLY TEMPERATURES AND PRECIPITATION FOR SELECTED CITIES   High **Low** (°F) Precipitation (in.)

	Jan	Feb	Mar	Apr	May	Jun	Jul	Aug	Sep	Oct	Nov	Dec
Baghdad, Iraq	61 39 1.1	64 43 1.1	72 48 1.1	84 57 0.7	97 66 0.3	106 73 0.0	109 75 0.0	109 75 0.0	104 70 0.0	91 61 0.1	77 52 0.8	64 43 1.0
Cairo, Egypt	64 46 0.2	70 48 0.2	75 52 0.2	82 57 0.1	91 63 0.0	95 68 0.0	97 70 0.0	95 72 0.0	90 68 0.0	86 64 0.0	79 57 0.1	68 50 0.2
Damascus, Syria	54 36 1.5	57 39 1.2	64 43 0.9	75 48 0.5	84 55 0.2	91 61 0.0	97 64 0.0	99 64 0.0	91 61 0.0	81 54 0.4	66 46 1.0	55 39 1.6
Istanbul, Turkey	46 37 3.6	48 36 2.7	52 37 2.4	61 45 1.6	70 54 1.2	77 61 1.1	82 64 0.9	82 66 1.2	75 61 1.9	68 55 2.6	59 48 3.6	52 41 4.4
Jerusalem, Israel	55 41 5.5	55 43 4.3	64 46 4.5	73 50 0.7	81 57 0.2	84 61 0.0	88 63 0.0	88 64 0.0	84 63 0.0	81 59 0.4	70 54 2.7	59 45 5.0
Kabul, Afghanistan	36 18 1.3	39 21 2.1	54 34 2.7	66 43 2.6	79 52 0.8	88 55 0.0	91 61 0.2	91 59 0.0	84 52 0.1	73 43 0.2	63 34 0.4	46 27 0.8
Karachi, Pakistan	77 55 0.3	79 57 0.4	84 66 0.4	90 73 0.1	93 79 0.0	93 82 0.4	91 81 3.5	88 79 2.3	88 77 1.1	91 72 0.1	88 64 0.1	81 57 0.2
Khartoum, Sudan	90 59 0.0	93 61 0.0	100 66 0.0	106 72 0.0	108 77 0.2	106 79 0.3	100 77 1.9	99 75 2.7	102 77 0.8	104 75 0.2	97 68 0.0	91 63 0.0
Nicosia, Cyprus	59 41 2.7	61 41 2.0	66 45 1.4	75 50 0.8	84 57 1.0	93 64 0.4	99 70 0.0	99 70 0.1	91 64 0.2	82 57 0.9	72 50 1.6	63 45 2.9
Tehran, Iran	45 27 1.7	50 32 1.4	59 39 1.5	72 48 1.3	82 57 0.6	93 66 0.1	99 72 0.1	97 72 0.1	90 64 0.1	75 54 0.4	63 43 0.9	52 34 1.2

Fahrenheit to Celsius conversion: subtract 32, then multiply by 5/9 (.55); Inches to centimeters: multiply by 2.54

Land Cover

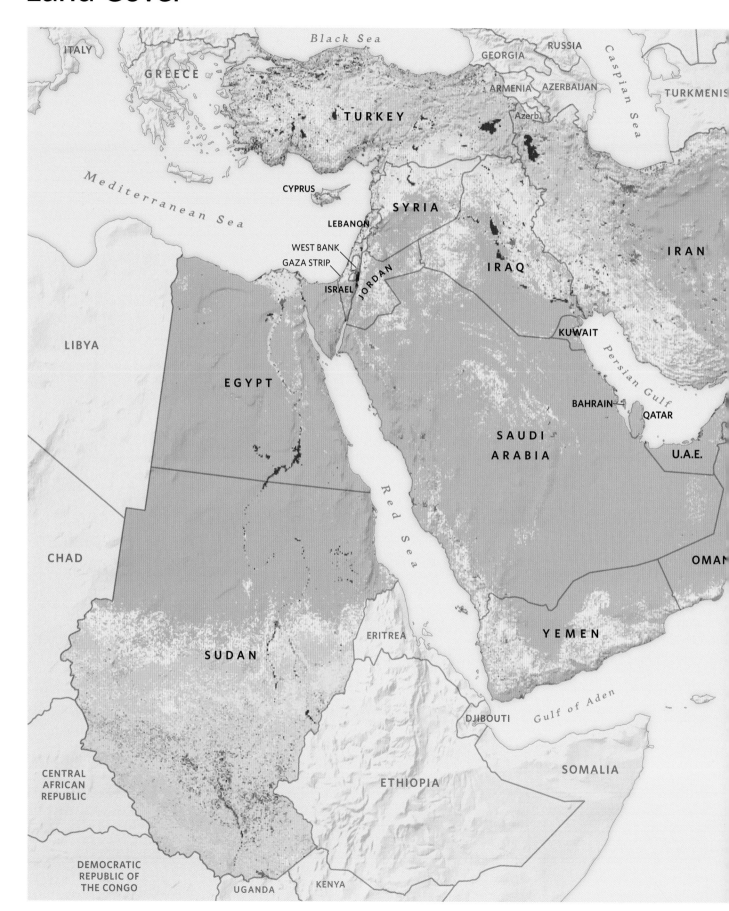

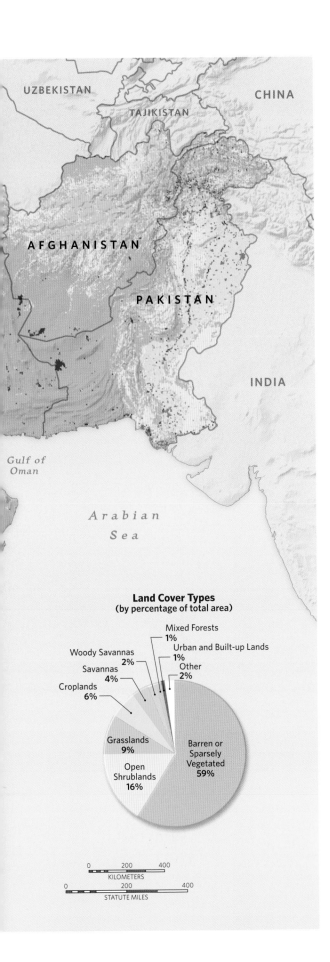

Land Cover Types
(by percentage of total area)

Mixed Forests 1%
Urban and Built-up Lands 1%
Woody Savannas 2%
Other 2%
Savannas 4%
Croplands 6%
Grasslands 9%
Barren or Sparsely Vegetated 59%
Open Shrublands 16%

0   200   400
KILOMETERS

0   200   400
STATUTE MILES

Natural Vegetation

EVERGREEN NEEDLELEAF FORESTS Lands dominated by needle-leaf woody vegetation and height exceeding 2 meters. Almost all trees remain green all year. Canopy is never without green foliage.

DECIDUOUS BROADLEAF FORESTS Lands dominated by woody vegetation and height exceeding 2 meters. Consists of broadleaf tree communities with an annual cycle of leaf-on and leaf-off periods.

MIXED FORESTS Lands dominated by trees and height exceeding 2 meters. Consists of tree communities with interspersed mixtures or mosaics of the other forest types.

CLOSED SHRUBLANDS Lands with woody vegetation less than 2 meters tall and with shrub canopy cover greater than 60 percent. The shrub foliage can be either evergreen or deciduous.

OPEN SHRUBLANDS Lands with woody vegetation less than 2 meters tall and with shrub canopy cover between 10–60 percent. The shrub foliage can be either evergreen or deciduous.

WOODY SAVANNAS Lands with herbaceous and other understory systems, and with forest canopy cover between 30–60 percent. The forest cover height exceeds 2 meters.

SAVANNAS Lands with herbaceous and other understory systems, and with forest canopy cover between 10–30 percent. The forest cover height exceeds 2 meters.

GRASSLANDS Lands with herbaceous types of cover. Tree and shrub cover is less than 10 percent.

Developed and Mosaic Lands

CROPLANDS Lands covered with temporary crops followed by harvest and a bare soil period (e.g., single and multiple cropping systems). Does not include perennial woody crops.

URBAN AND BUILT-UP LANDS Lands dominated by buildings and other man-made structures.

CROPLAND/NATURAL VEGETATION MOSAICS Lands with a mosaic of croplands, forests, shrubland, and grasslands in which no one component comprises more than 60 percent of the landscape.

Non-Vegetated Areas

BARREN OR SPARSELY VEGETATED Lands with exposed soil, sand, rocks, or snow and never has more than 10 percent vegetated cover during any time of the year.

WATER BODIES Oceans, seas, lakes, reservoirs, and rivers. Can be either fresh or salt-water bodies.

Population

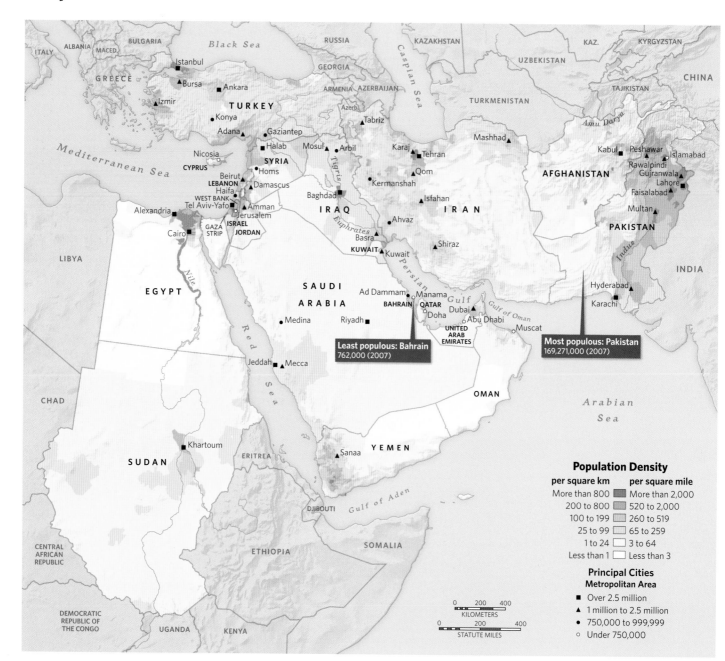

Least populous: Bahrain
762,000 (2007)

Most populous: Pakistan
169,271,000 (2007)

Population Density

per square km	per square mile
More than 800	More than 2,000
200 to 800	520 to 2,000
100 to 199	260 to 519
25 to 99	65 to 259
1 to 24	3 to 64
Less than 1	Less than 3

Principal Cities
Metropolitan Area

■ Over 2.5 million
▲ 1 million to 2.5 million
● 750,000 to 999,999
○ Under 750,000

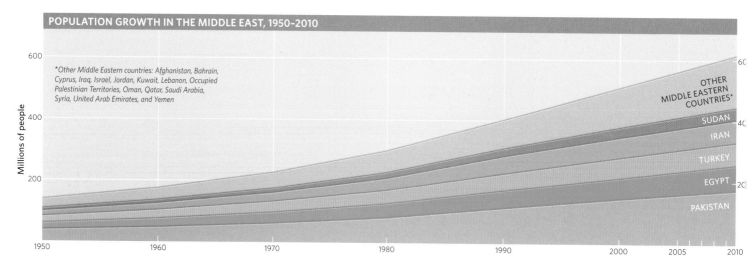

POPULATION GROWTH IN THE MIDDLE EAST, 1950–2010

*Other Middle Eastern countries: Afghanistan, Bahrain, Cyprus, Iraq, Israel, Jordan, Kuwait, Lebanon, Occupied Palestinian Territories, Oman, Qatar, Saudi Arabia, Syria, United Arab Emirates, and Yemen

OTHER MIDDLE EASTERN COUNTRIES*
SUDAN
IRAN
TURKEY
EGYPT
PAKISTAN

Millions of people

600

400

200

1950 1960 1970 1980 1990 2000 2005 2010

FERTILITY

Average number of children born to a woman in a given population. (World average: 2.7)

Afghanistan	7.5	Egypt	3.2
Yemen	6.0	Qatar	2.9
Occ. Pal. Terr.	5.6	Israel	2.9
Iraq	4.9	U.A.E.	2.5
Sudan	4.8	Bahrain	2.5
Pakistan	4.0	Lebanon	2.3
Saudi Arabia	3.8	Kuwait	2.3
Oman	3.7	Turkey	2.2
Jordan	3.5	Iran	2.1
Syria	3.5	Cyprus	1.6

LIFE EXPECTANCY

Life expectancy at birth, in years. (World average: 67.8)

Israel	80.3	Jordan	71.5
U.A.E.	78.5	Turkey	71.5
Cyprus	78.0	Lebanon	71.0
Kuwait	77.6	Egypt	70.6
Saudi Arabia	75.0	Iran	69.5
Oman	74.3	Pakistan	62.2
Bahrain	73.8	Yemen	60.3
Syria	73.1	Sudan	57.5
Qatar	72.7	Iraq	57.0
Occ. Pal. Terr.	72.3	Afghanistan	42.0

URBAN POPULATION

Percentage of population living in urban areas. (World average: 48.7%)

Kuwait	98.3	Cyprus	69.3
Bahrain	96.5	Turkey	67.3
Qatar	95.4	Iran	66.9
Israel	91.6	Iraq	66.9
Lebanon	86.6	Syria	50.6
Jordan	82.3	Egypt	42.8
Saudi Arabia	81.0	Sudan	40.8
U.A.E.	76.7	Pakistan	34.9
Occ. Pal. Terr.	71.6	Yemen	27.3
Oman	71.5	Afghanistan	22.9

MIGRANT POPULATION

Migrants as a percent of total population. (World average: 29.3%)

Qatar	80.0	Cyprus	13.9
U.A.E.	78.3	Syria	5.2
Kuwait	61.8	Iran	2.8
Occ. Pal. Terr.	44.7	Pakistan	2.1
Bahrain	40.8	Turkey	1.8
Jordan	40.1	Sudan	1.7
Israel	39.8	Yemen	1.3
Saudi Arabia	26.9	Egypt	0.2
Oman	25.0	Afghanistan	0.2
Lebanon	16.4	Iraq	0.1

POPULATION BY AGE AND GENDER

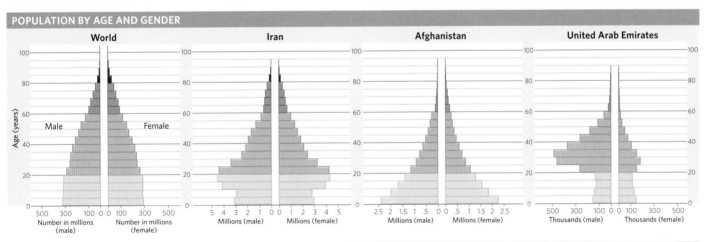

POPULATIONS OF MAJOR CITIES (METROPOLITAN AREA)

City	1950	2005	City	1950	2005
Karachi, Pakistan	1,047,000	11,608,000	Jeddah, Saudi Arabia	119,000	2,860,000
Cairo, Egypt	2,494,000	11,128,000	Halab, Syria	319,000	2,520,000
Istanbul, Turkey	967,000	9,712,000	Faisalabad, Pakistan	168,000	2,494,000
Tehran, Iran	1,041,000	7,314,000	Izmir, Turkey	224,000	2,487,000
Lahore, Pakistan	836,000	6,289,000	Damascus, Syria	367,000	2,272,000
Baghdad, Iraq	579,000	5,904,000	Mashhad, Iran	173,000	2,134,000
Khartoum, Sudan	183,000	4,518,000	Basra, Iraq	116,000	2,005,000
Riyadh, Saudi Arabia	111,000	4,193,000	Kuwait, Kuwait	81,000	1,810,000
Alexandria, Egypt	1,037,000	3,770,000	Sanaa, Yemen	46,000	1,801,000
Ankara, Turkey	281,000	3,573,000	Beirut, Lebanon	322,000	1,777,000
Tel Aviv-Yafo, Israel	418,000	3,012,000	Rawalpindi, Pakistan	233,000	1,770,000
Kabul, Afghanistan	171,000	2,994,000	Isfahan, Iran	184,000	1,535,000

Urbanization

**Population of Urban Areas
Over 4 Million People, 2005**
(in millions)

35
20
10
5

Moving On Up?

Urbanization was born in the Middle East. Around 4000 B.C., the Sumerians of Mesopotamia had adopted advanced farming techniques (especially irrigation), enabling them to become the first civilization that could afford to employ the majority of its people in non-agricultural activities. Six thousand years later the world has caught up, becoming majority urban in 2007. The sheer number of migrants seeking better lives in cities in the Middle East and around the world today is causing new problems. Some cities can't provide enough services for their ballooning outskirts, fueling more slums and poverty than opportunities.

FASTEST GROWING CITIES IN THE MIDDLE EAST

Average annual rate of change for cities with 750,000 inhabitants or more, 2000-2005

City	Rate	City	Rate
Kabul, Afghanistan	8.4	**Medina**, Saudi Arabia	3.5
Dubai, United Arab Emirates	7.0	**Konya**, Turkey	3.4
Sanaa, Yemen	5.5	**Gaziantep**, Turkey	3.2
Ad Dammam, Saudi Arabia	3.6	**Gujranwala**, Pakistan	3.2
Arbil, Iraq	3.6	**Riyadh**, Saudi Arabia	3.2
Beirut, Lebanon	3.6	**Kuwait**, Kuwait	3.1
Bursa, Turkey	3.6	**Mosul**, Iraq	3.1

PERCENT OF POPULATION LIVING IN URBAN AREAS, 1950-2010

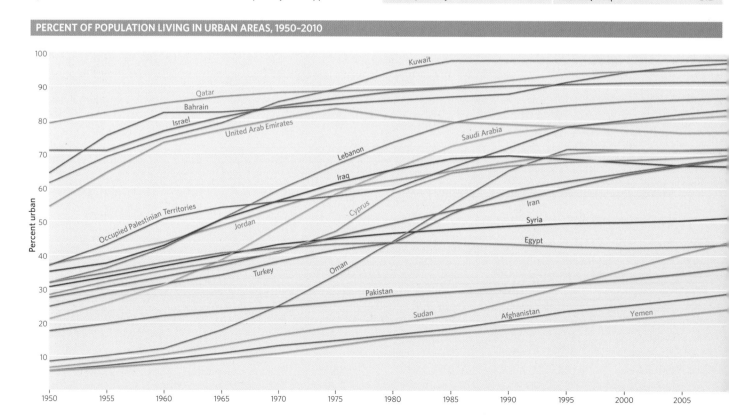

Dubai: Sudden City

Sites under construction are shown as (U/C).

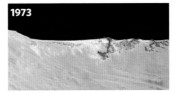
Palm Jumeirah

Human Impact

Dubai's new and exotic man-made islands—some in the shape of palm trees—have been created to accommodate the wealthiest of its new residents. The first to be built, the Palm Jumeirah, offered beachfront lots for 4,000 villas and apartments; buyers snapped up every site within just 72 hours. Other similar projects have followed, with waterfront properties bringing in large amounts of cash (they've sold for 7 to 30 million dollars each)—but at a cost to the planet. Environmentalists point out the resultant losses to coral, turtle nesting sites, and the upset marine ecology of the Persian Gulf.

Quiet Village to Booming City

Not long ago Dubai was a sleepy, sun-scorched village occupied by pearl divers, fishermen, and traders who docked their boats along a narrow creek that snaked through town. But in 1959, then-ruler Sheikh Rashid bin Saeed al Maktoum began to work toward a new vision, borrowing many millions of dollars from Kuwait and constructing a whole new infrastructure. The creek was dredged until it was wide and deep enough for ships. New wharves and warehouses were built, and plans were made for roads, schools, and homes. Now, just five decades later, Dubai is a floodlit, air-conditioned, skyscrapered fantasy land of a million people. With its Manhattan-style skyline (including the Burj Dubai, the tallest building

in the world), world-class port, and colossal, duty-free shopping malls, Dubai now attracts more tourists than all of India. It also attracts more shipping vessels than Singapore, and more foreign capital than many European countries. People from 150 countries have moved here to live and work. The city's economic growth rate, 16 percent, is nearly double that of flourishing China. A success story on many levels, it is not without troubles—including the plight of tens of thousands of guest workers who live in squalid conditions, earning an average laborer's wage of about five dollars per day. Dubai is a place like nowhere else, a land of sharp contrasts and big dreams, and a vibrant new hub of the Middle East.

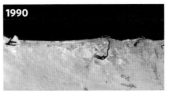
1973

1990

2006

Dubai's unique growth as seen from orbit

The Burj Dubai, tallest building in the world

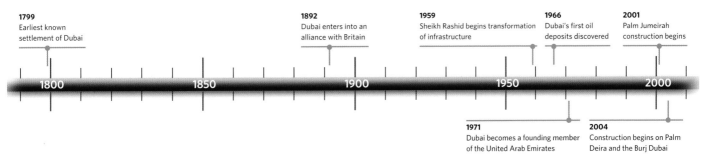

1799
Earliest known settlement of Dubai

1892
Dubai enters into an alliance with Britain

1959
Sheikh Rashid begins transformation of infrastructure

1966
Dubai's first oil deposits discovered

2001
Palm Jumeirah construction begins

1800   1850   1900   1950   2000

1971
Dubai becomes a founding member of the United Arab Emirates

2004
Construction begins on Palm Deira and the Burj Dubai

Religion

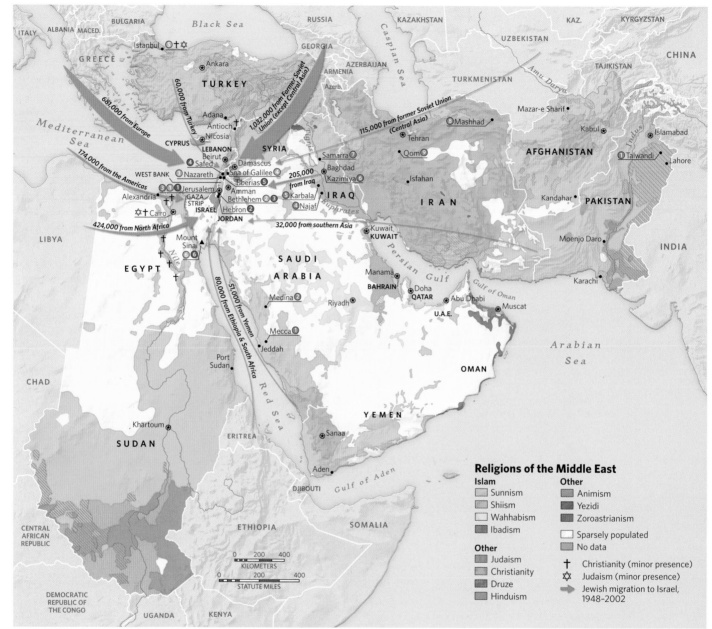

Religions of the Middle East

Islam
- Sunnism
- Shiism
- Wahhabism
- Ibadism

Other
- Judaism
- Christianity
- Druze
- Hinduism

Other
- Animism
- Yezidi
- Zoroastrianism
- Sparsely populated
- No data

† Christianity (minor presence)
✡ Judaism (minor presence)
➡ Jewish migration to Israel, 1948-2002

PRIMARY SOURCE: *M.R. Izady (except Pakistan)*

SACRED SITES IN THE MIDDLE EAST

Christian

1 **Jerusalem:** Church of the Holy Sepulchre, Jesus' crucifixion

2 **Bethlehem:** Jesus' birthplace

3 **Nazareth:** Hometown of Jesus Christ

4 **Sea of Galilee:** Where Jesus gave the Sermon on the Mount

5 **Istanbul (Constantinople):** Dedicated as the capital of the newly-Christian Roman Empire (A.D. 300) by Constantine the Great

6 **Mount Sinai:** Site of God's manifestation to Moses and the revelation of the Ten Commandments given to him by God

Jewish

1 **Jerusalem:** Location of the Western Wall and first and second temples; City of David; the ancient and modern capital of Israel

2 **Hebron:** Burial spot of patriarchs and matriarchs

3 **Bethlehem:** Site of Rachel's tomb

4 **Safed:** Where Kabbalah (Jewish mysticism) flourished

5 **Tiberias:** Where Talmud (source of Jewish law) was first composed

6 **Mount Sinai:** Site of God's revelation, where God appeared to Moses and gave him the Ten Commandments

Muslim

1 **Mecca:** The Prophet Muhammad's birthplace; destination of the pilgrimage, or hajj; houses the Kaaba (shrine that Muslims face when praying)

2 **Medina:** Burial place of the Prophet Muhammad; contains the tombs of the 2nd, 4th, 5th, and 6th Shiite Imams

3 **Jerusalem:** The first Qibla (direction of prayers) of Islam before being replaced by Mecca; site of a night-long ascension of the Prophet Muhammad to the heavens

4 **Najaf** (Shiite): Tomb of the first Imam, Ali; ancient center of Shiite learning; known as the "Vatican City" of Shiism

5 **Karbala** (Shiite): Tomb of the 3rd Imam and martyr, Hussein

Muslim (continued)

6 **Kazimiya** (Shiite): Tombs of the 7th and 9th Imams (located inside metropolitan Baghdad)

7 **Samarra** (Shiite): Tombs of the 10th and 11th Imams; where the 12th Imam, the Mahdi, went into occultation

8 **Mashhad** (Shiite): Tomb of the 8th Imam, Rida/Reza; one of the three primary centers of Shiite learning

9 **Qom** (Shiite): Tomb of Fatima (8th Imam's sister); one of the three primary centers of Shiite learning

Other

1 **Talwandi:** Founder of Sikhism, Guru Nanak, was born here in 1469

RELIGIOUS ADHERENTS IN THE MIDDLE EAST*

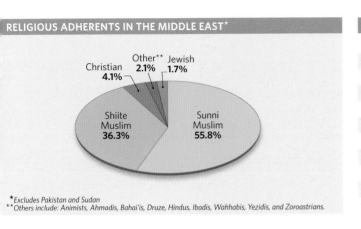

*Excludes Pakistan and Sudan
**Others include: Animists, Ahmadis, Bahai'is, Druze, Hindus, Ibadis, Wahhabis, Yezidis, and Zoroastrians.

TOP 10 NATIONAL MUSLIM POPULATIONS

	Muslim population	% of total population
1. Indonesia	199,845,000	88.0%
2. Pakistan	164,193,000	97.0%
3. India	150,951,000	13.7%
4. Bangladesh	125,573,000	88.5%
5. Turkey	73,819,000	99.8%
6. Iran	69,784,000	98.0%
7. Egypt	66,076,000	90.0%
8. Nigeria	55,351,000	42.1%
9. Algeria	31,831,000	96.9%
10. Morocco	30,887,000	98.5%

TOP 10 NATIONAL JEWISH POPULATIONS

	Jewish population	% of total population
1. United States	5,729,000	1.9%
2. Israel	5,613,000	76.4%
3. France	605,000	1.0%
4. Argentina	513,000	1.3%
5. West Bank	458,000	17.0%
6. Canada	418,000	1.3%
7. United Kingdom	280,000	0.5%
8. Germany	225,000	0.3%
9. Russia	187,000	0.1%
10. Ukraine	181,000	0.4%

BRANCHES OF ISLAM IN THE MIDDLE EAST*

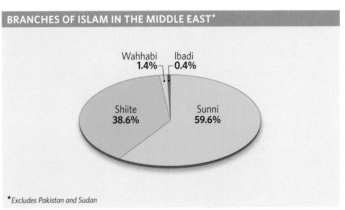

*Excludes Pakistan and Sudan

RELIGIOUS ADHERENTS BY POLITICAL AREA

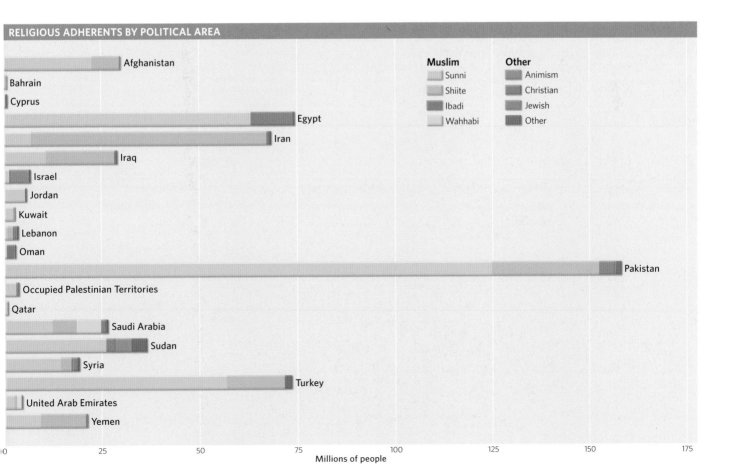

Language and Ethnic Groups

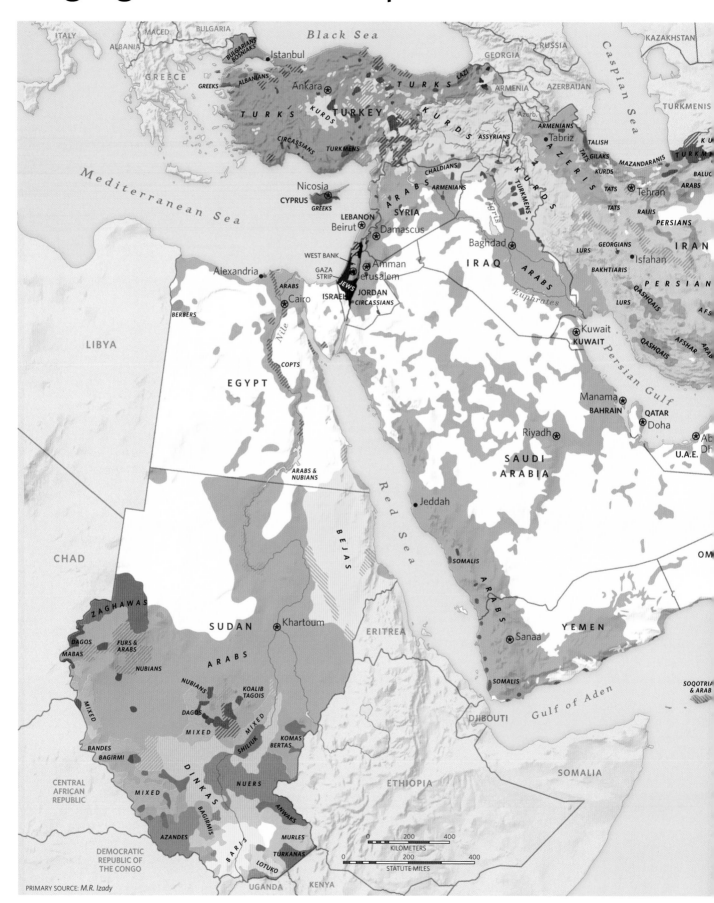

ITALY
ALBANIA
MACED.
BULGARIA
Black Sea
GEORGIA
RUSSIA
KAZAKHSTAN
GREECE
BULGARIANS
BOSNIAKS
Istanbul
ALBANIANS
LAZI
ARMENIA
AZERBAIJAN
TURKMENIS.
Caspian Sea
GREEKS
T U R K S
Ankara ✪
T U R K S
CIRCASSIANS
KURDS
TURKEY
KURDS
ARMENIANS
ASSYRIANS
Azerb.
ARMENIANS
TALISH
GILAKS
TATS
MAZANDARANIS
TURKM.
TURKMENS
TURKMENS
KURDS
KURDS
TATS
BALUC.
Mediterranean Sea
Nicosia
CYPRUS
GREEKS
CHALDIANS
ARMENIANS
A R A B S
SYRIA
Damascus ✪
RAIJIS
TATS
Tehran ✪
ARABS
PERSIANS
LEBANON
Beirut ✪
Baghdad ✪
IRAQ
GEORGIANS
I R A N
WEST BANK
Amman ✪
LURS
Isfahan •
Alexandria •
ARABS
GAZA
STRIP
JEWS
Jerusalem ✪
JORDAN
ISRAEL
CIRCASSIANS
A R A B S
Euphrates
BAKHTIARIS
P E R S I A N
Cairo ✪
BERBERS
LURS
QASHQAIS
AFS.
LIBYA
COPTS
Kuwait ✪
KUWAIT
QASHQAIS
AFSHAR
EGYPT
Manama ✪
BAHRAIN
QATAR
Doha
Ab.
Dh.
U.A.E.
Riyadh ✪
SAUDI
ARABIA
Red Sea
CHAD
ARABS &
NUBIANS
Jeddah •
OM.
B E J A S
SOMALIS
A R A B S
ZAGHAWAS
SUDAN
Khartoum ✪
ERITREA
YEMEN
DAGOS
FURS &
ARABS
MABAS
A R A B S
Sanaa ✪
NUBIANS
NUBIANS
KOALIB
TAGOIS
SOMALIS
SOQOTRIA
& ARAB.
MIXED
DAGOS
MIXED
MIXED
KOMAS
BERTAS
DJIBOUTI
Gulf of Aden
BANDES
BAGIRMI
SHILLUK
MIXED
D I N K A S
NUERS
SOMALIA
CENTRAL
AFRICAN
REPUBLIC
MIXED
ANWAKS
ETHIOPIA
BAGIRMIS
AZANDES
B A R I S
MURLES
TURKANAS
DEMOCRATIC
REPUBLIC
OF
THE CONGO
LOTUKO
UGANDA
KENYA

0   200   400
KILOMETERS
0   200   400
STATUTE MILES

PRIMARY SOURCE: *M.R. Izady*

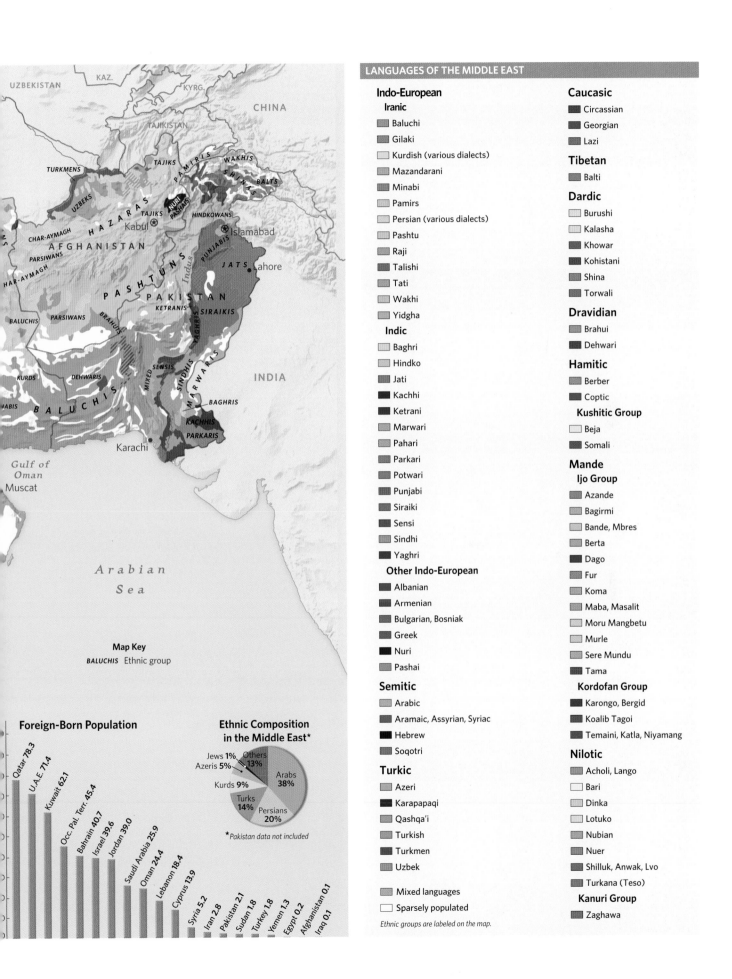

UZBEKISTAN
KAZ.
KYRG.
CHINA
TAJIKISTAN
TURKMENS
TAJIKS
PAMIRIS
WAKHIS
SHINAS
UZBEKS
BALTS
HAZARAS
NURI
PASHAIS
CHAR-AYMAGH
TAJIKS
HINDKOWANS
AFGHANISTAN
Kabul
Islamabad
PARSIWANS
PUNJABIS
HAR-AYMAGH
PASHTUNS
Indus
JATS
Lahore
BALUCHIS
PARSIWANS
PAKISTAN
BRAHUIS
KETRANIS
SIRAIKIS
KURDS
DEHWARIS
MIXED
SENSIS
YAGHRIS
SINDHIS
MARWARIS
INDIA
ABIS
BALUCHIS
BAGHRIS
KACHHIS
PARKARIS
Karachi

Gulf of Oman
Muscat

Arabian Sea

Map Key
BALUCHIS Ethnic group

Foreign-Born Population

Qatar 78.3
U.A.E. 71.4
Kuwait 62.1
Occ. Pal. Terr. 45.4
Bahrain 40.7
Israel 39.6
Jordan 39.0
Saudi Arabia 25.9
Oman 24.4
Lebanon 18.4
Cyprus 13.9
Syria 5.2
Iran 2.8
Pakistan 2.1
Sudan 1.8
Turkey 1.8
Yemen 1.3
Egypt 0.2
Afghanistan 0.1
Iraq 0.1

Ethnic Composition in the Middle East*

Jews 1%
Others 13%
Azeris 5%
Arabs 38%
Kurds 9%
Turks 14%
Persians 20%

*Pakistan data not included

LANGUAGES OF THE MIDDLE EAST

Indo-European
Iranic
- Baluchi
- Gilaki
- Kurdish (various dialects)
- Mazandarani
- Minabi
- Pamirs
- Persian (various dialects)
- Pashtu
- Raji
- Talishi
- Tati
- Wakhi
- Yidgha

Indic
- Baghri
- Hindko
- Jati
- Kachhi
- Ketrani
- Marwari
- Pahari
- Parkari
- Potwari
- Punjabi
- Siraiki
- Sensi
- Sindhi
- Yaghri

Other Indo-European
- Albanian
- Armenian
- Bulgarian, Bosniak
- Greek
- Nuri
- Pashai

Semitic
- Arabic
- Aramaic, Assyrian, Syriac
- Hebrew
- Soqotri

Turkic
- Azeri
- Karapapaqi
- Qashqa'i
- Turkish
- Turkmen
- Uzbek

- Mixed languages
- Sparsely populated

Ethnic groups are labeled on the map.

Caucasic
- Circassian
- Georgian
- Lazi

Tibetan
- Balti

Dardic
- Burushi
- Kalasha
- Khowar
- Kohistani
- Shina
- Torwali

Dravidian
- Brahui
- Dehwari

Hamitic
- Berber
- Coptic

Kushitic Group
- Beja
- Somali

Mande
Ijo Group
- Azande
- Bagirmi
- Bande, Mbres
- Berta
- Dago
- Fur
- Koma
- Maba, Masalit
- Moru Mangbetu
- Murle
- Sere Mundu
- Tama

Kordofan Group
- Karongo, Bergid
- Koalib Tagoi
- Temaini, Katla, Niyamang

Nilotic
- Acholi, Lango
- Bari
- Dinka
- Lotuko
- Nubian
- Nuer
- Shilluk, Anwak, Lvo
- Turkana (Teso)

Kanuri Group
- Zaghawa

Oil

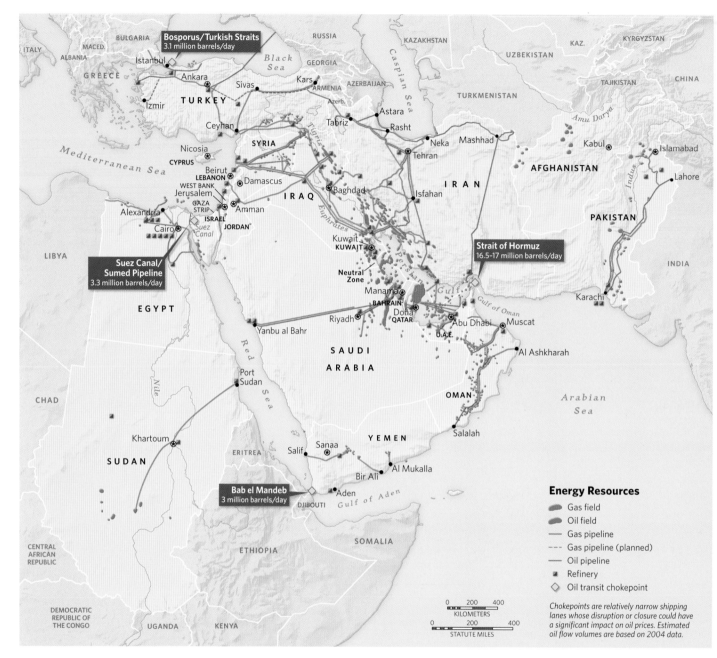

Bosporus/Turkish Straits
3.1 million barrels/day

Strait of Hormuz
16.5-17 million barrels/day

Suez Canal/ Sumed Pipeline
3.3 million barrels/day

Bab el Mandeb
3 million barrels/day

Energy Resources

- Gas field
- Oil field
- —— Gas pipeline
- --- Gas pipeline (planned)
- —— Oil pipeline
- ▪ Refinery
- ◇ Oil transit chokepoint

Chokepoints are relatively narrow shipping lanes whose disruption or closure could have a significant impact on oil prices. Estimated oil flow volumes are based on 2004 data.

| 0 | 200 | 400 |
KILOMETERS

| 0 | 200 | 400 |
STATUTE MILES

OIL RESERVES IN THE MIDDLE EAST

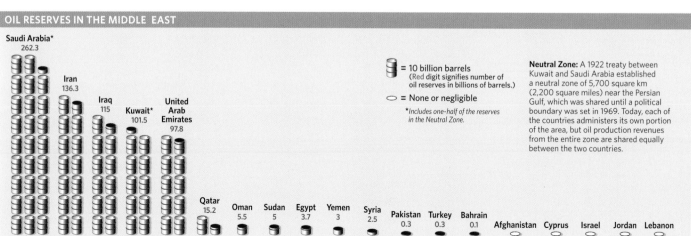

Saudi Arabia*
262.3

Iran
136.3

Iraq
115

Kuwait*
101.5

United Arab Emirates
97.8

Qatar
15.2

Oman
5.5

Sudan
5

Egypt
3.7

Yemen
3

Syria
2.5

Pakistan
0.3

Turkey
0.3

Bahrain
0.1

Afghanistan

Cyprus

Israel

Jordan

Lebanon

= 10 billion barrels
(Red digit signifies number of oil reserves in billions of barrels.)

= None or negligible

*Includes one-half of the reserves in the Neutral Zone.

Neutral Zone: A 1922 treaty between Kuwait and Saudi Arabia established a neutral zone of 5,700 square km (2,200 square miles) near the Persian Gulf, which was shared until a political boundary was set in 1969. Today, each of the countries administers its own portion of the area, but oil production revenues from the entire zone are shared equally between the two countries.

REGIONAL SHARE OF WORLD OIL RESERVES

All figures are shown in barrels.

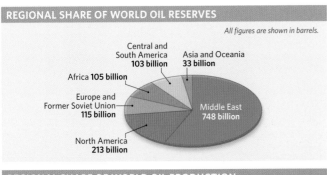

Central and South America **103 billion**

Asia and Oceania **33 billion**

Africa **105 billion**

Europe and Former Soviet Union **115 billion**

Middle East **748 billion**

North America **213 billion**

REGIONAL SHARE OF WORLD OIL PRODUCTION

All figures are shown in barrels per day.

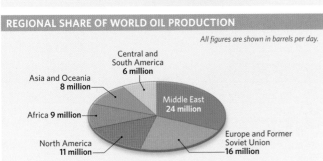

Central and South America **6 million**

Asia and Oceania **8 million**

Middle East **24 million**

Africa **9 million**

North America **11 million**

Europe and Former Soviet Union **16 million**

LEADING CRUDE OIL PRODUCERS IN THE MIDDLE EAST, 1970-2006

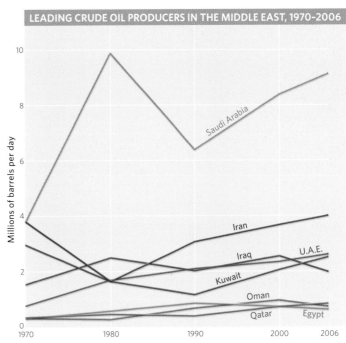

Millions of barrels per day

Saudi Arabia

Iran

Iraq   U.A.E.

Kuwait

Oman

Qatar   Egypt

1970   1980   1990   2000   2006

MIDDLE EAST EXPORTS AND GLOBAL OIL CONSUMPTION

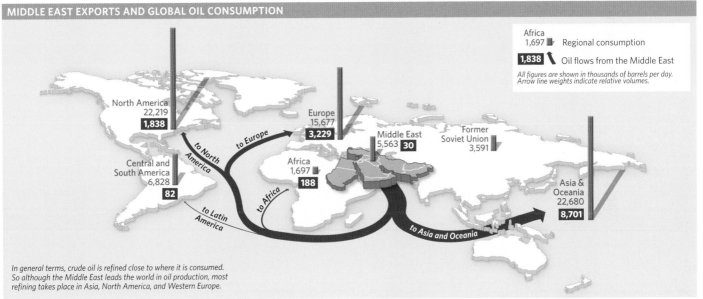

Africa 1,697 — Regional consumption

1,838 — Oil flows from the Middle East

All figures are shown in thousands of barrels per day. Arrow line weights indicate relative volumes.

North America 22,219 | **1,838**

Europe 15,677 | **3,229**

Middle East 5,563 | **30**

Former Soviet Union 3,591

Central and South America 6,828 | **82**

Africa 1,697 | **188**

Asia & Oceania 22,680 | **8,701**

to Europe
to North America
to Latin America
to Africa
to Asia and Oceania

In general terms, crude oil is refined close to where it is consumed. So although the Middle East leads the world in oil production, most refining takes place in Asia, North America, and Western Europe.

TOP OIL PRODUCERS, WORLDWIDE

2006 data. Figures listed in thousands of barrels per day.

Russia	9,247	Iraq	1,996
Saudi Arabia	9,152	Algeria	1,814
United States	5,136	Brazil	1,723
Iran	4,028	Libya	1,681
China	3,686	United Kingdom	1,490
Mexico	3,256	Angola	1,420
United Arab Emirates	2,636	Kazakhstan	1,100
Kuwait	2,535	Indonesia	1,019
Canada	2,525	Qatar	850
Venezuela	2,511	Oman	738
Norway	2,491	Argentina	697
Nigeria	2,440	India	689

TOP OIL CONSUMERS, WORLDWIDE

2006 data. Figures listed in thousands of barrels per day.

United States	20,588	Australia	921
China	7,274	Turkey	619
Japan	5,222	Belgium	559
Germany	2,630	Poland	495
Canada	2,201	Greece	435
South Korea	2,158	Sweden	363
Mexico	2,030	Portugal	305
France	1,972	Austria	284
United Kingdom	1,815	Switzerland	282
Italy	1,709	Norway	242
Spain	1,584	Finland	225
Netherlands	1,013	Czech Republic	209

Water

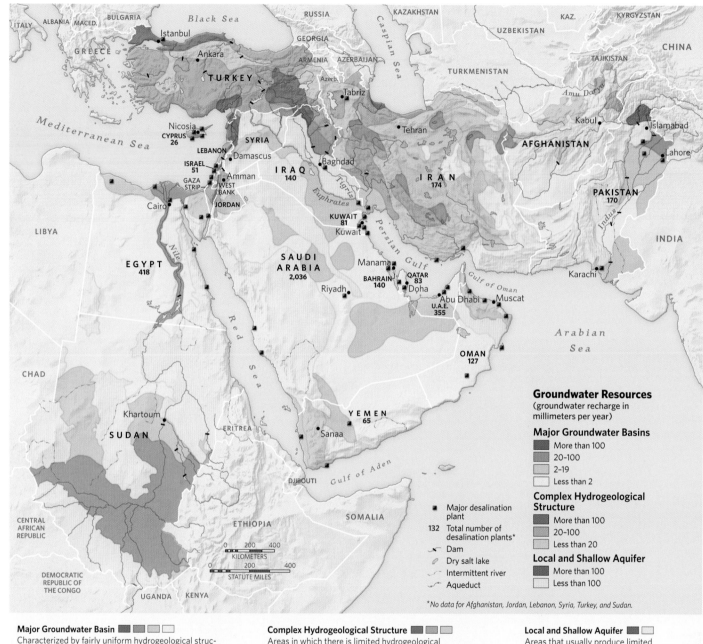

Groundwater Resources
(groundwater recharge in millimeters per year)

Major Groundwater Basins
- More than 100
- 20–100
- 2–19
- Less than 2

Complex Hydrogeological Structure
- More than 100
- 20–100
- Less than 20

Local and Shallow Aquifer
- More than 100
- Less than 100

- ■ Major desalination plant
- 132 Total number of desalination plants*
- ⌐ Dam
- ⌀ Dry salt lake
- Intermittent river
- Aqueduct

*No data for Afghanistan, Jordan, Lebanon, Syria, Turkey, and Sudan.

Major Groundwater Basin
Characterized by fairly uniform hydrogeological structures filled with groundwater-soaked sediments; may offer good conditions for water withdrawal.

Complex Hydrogeological Structure
Areas in which there is limited hydrogeological consistency and the groundwater potential varies widely. These areas often coincide with fault zones.

Local and Shallow Aquifer
Areas that usually produce limited groundwater supply.

RENEWABLE FRESH WATER IN THE MIDDLE EAST*

Renewable fresh water figures shown in km³ per year. World average: 322.2

Country	km³	Country	km³
Turkey	234.0	Saudi Arabia	2.4
Pakistan	233.8	Israel	1.7
Sudan	154.0	Oman	1.0
Iran	137.5	Jordan	0.9
Iraq	96.4	Cyprus	0.4
Egypt	86.8	U.A.E.	0.2
Afghanistan	65.0	Bahrain	0.1
Syria	46.1	Qatar	.05
Lebanon	4.8	Kuwait	.02
Yemen	4.1		

*These data reflect average long-term renewable water resources, typically comprised of both surface water and groundwater supplies, including surface inflows from neighboring countries. Flows to other countries are not subtracted from these numbers.

FRESH WATER WITHDRAWALS IN THE MIDDLE EAST*

Fresh water withdrawal figures in km³ per year. World average: 25.0

Country	km³	Country	km³
Pakistan	169.4	U.A.E.	2.3
Iran	72.9	Israel	2.1
Egypt	68.3	Lebanon	1.4
Iraq	42.7	Oman	1.4
Turkey	39.8	Jordan	1.0
Sudan	37.3	Kuwait	0.4
Afghanistan	23.3	Bahrain	0.3
Syria	20.0	Qatar	0.3
Saudi Arabia	17.3	Cyprus	0.2
Yemen	6.6		

*Fresh water "withdrawal" typically refers to water taken from a water source for use. It does not refer to water "consumed" in that use.

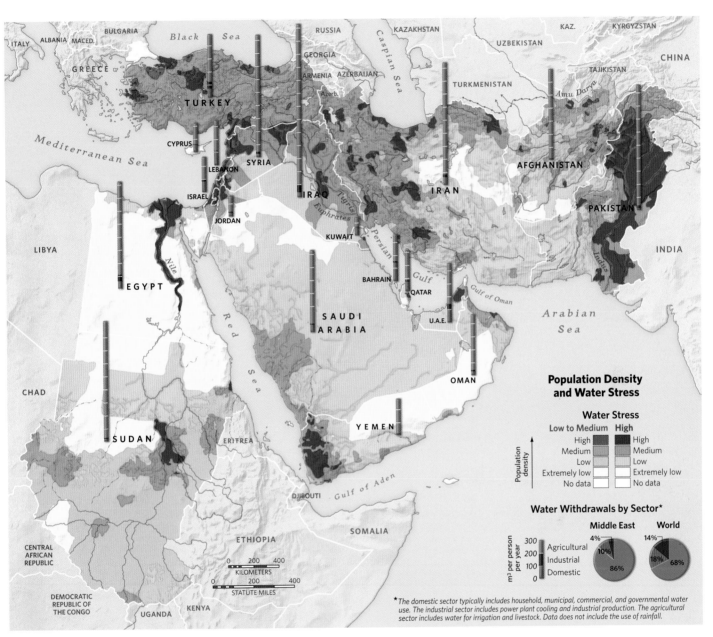

Population Density and Water Stress

Water Stress

Low to Medium	High
High	High
Medium	Medium
Low	Low
Extremely low	Extremely low
No data	No data

Population density

Water Withdrawals by Sector*

Middle East — Agricultural 86%, Industrial 10%, Domestic 4%

World — Agricultural 68%, Industrial 18%, Domestic 14%

m³ per person per year: 300, 200, 100, 0

*The domestic sector typically includes household, municipal, commercial, and governmental water use. The industrial sector includes power plant cooling and industrial production. The agricultural sector includes water for irrigation and livestock. Data does not include the use of rainfall.

KILOMETERS 0 200 400
STATUTE MILES 0 200 400

SEVERE WATER STRESS: WATER USE AS A PERCENT OF SUPPLY

Middle Eastern countries whose water use exceeds 40% of annual renewable supply (severe water stress) are listed below.

Kuwait	2,200	Yemen	162	Pakistan	72
U.A.E.	1,533	Oman	138	Cyprus	53
Saudi Arabia	722	Israel	121	Iran	53
Qatar	547	Jordan	115	Iraq	44
Bahrain	259	Egypt	79	Syria	43

ACCESS TO IMPROVED DRINKING WATER

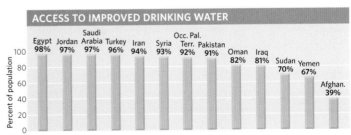

Egypt 98%, Jordan 97%, Saudi Arabia 97%, Turkey 96%, Iran 94%, Syria 93%, Occ. Pal. Terr. 92%, Pakistan 91%, Oman 82%, Iraq 81%, Sudan 70%, Yemen 67%, Afghan. 39%

Percent of population

FRESH WATER WITHDRAWALS, WORLDWIDE (TOP 10)

Fresh water withdrawals shown in km³ per year.

India	645.8	Indonesia	82.8
China	549.8	Thailand	82.8
United States	477.0	Bangladesh	79.4
Pakistan	169.4	Mexico	78.2
Japan	88.4	Russia	76.7

DESALINATION CAPACITY, WORLDWIDE (TOP 10)

Capacity figures shown in m³ per day.

Saudi Arabia	7,245,901	Japan	1,368,354
United States	6,616,289	Qatar	920,035
U.A.E.	5,456,027	Libya	887,835
Spain	2,379,299	South Korea	870,240
Kuwait	2,080,957	Italy	725,907

Note: Please see the inside back cover for metric conversions.

Food and Agriculture

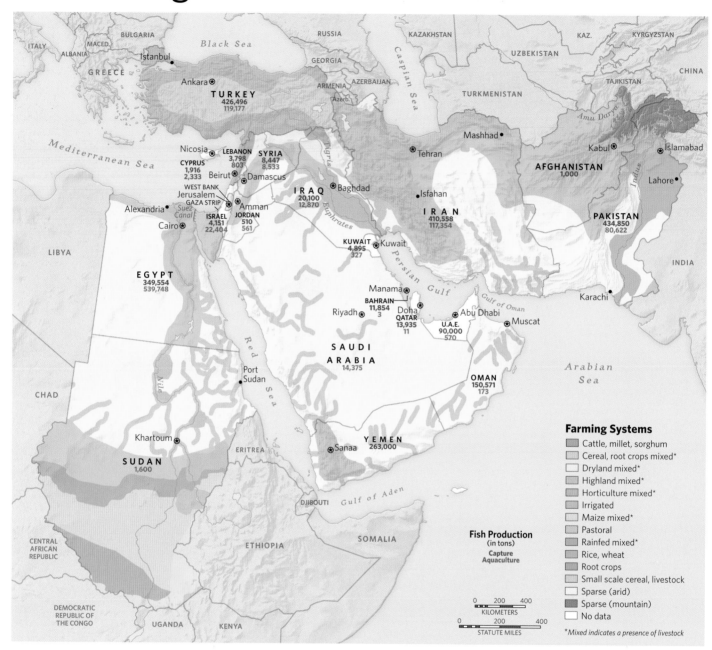

Farming Systems
- Cattle, millet, sorghum
- Cereal, root crops mixed*
- Dryland mixed*
- Highland mixed*
- Horticulture mixed*
- Irrigated
- Maize mixed*
- Pastoral
- Rainfed mixed*
- Rice, wheat
- Root crops
- Small scale cereal, livestock
- Sparse (arid)
- Sparse (mountain)
- No data

*Mixed indicates a presence of livestock

Fish Production
(in tons)
Capture
Aquaculture

Map country values:
- TURKEY 426,496 / 119,177
- CYPRUS 1,916 / 2,333
- LEBANON 3,798 / 803
- SYRIA 8,447 / 8,533
- ISRAEL 4,151 / 22,404
- JORDAN 510 / 561
- IRAQ 20,100 / 12,870
- IRAN 410,558 / 117,354
- KUWAIT 4,895 / 327
- EGYPT 349,554 / 539,748
- BAHRAIN 11,854 / 3
- QATAR 13,935 / 11
- U.A.E. 90,000 / 570
- SAUDI ARABIA 14,375
- OMAN 150,571 / 173
- YEMEN 263,000
- SUDAN 1,600
- AFGHANISTAN 1,000
- PAKISTAN 434,850 / 80,622

SOURCES OF DIETARY ENERGY CONSUMPTION

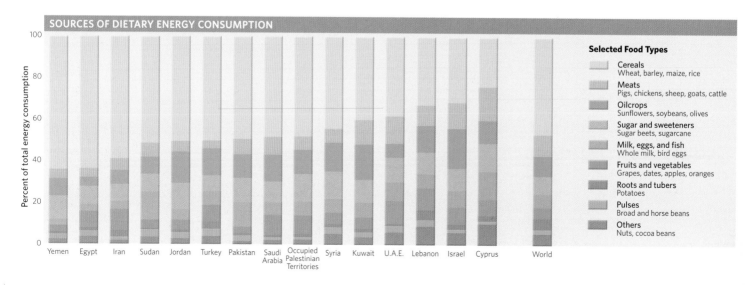

Percent of total energy consumption

Countries: Yemen, Egypt, Iran, Sudan, Jordan, Turkey, Pakistan, Saudi Arabia, Occupied Palestinian Territories, Syria, Kuwait, U.A.E., Lebanon, Israel, Cyprus, World

Selected Food Types
- Cereals — Wheat, barley, maize, rice
- Meats — Pigs, chickens, sheep, goats, cattle
- Oilcrops — Sunflowers, soybeans, olives
- Sugar and sweeteners — Sugar beets, sugarcane
- Milk, eggs, and fish — Whole milk, bird eggs
- Fruits and vegetables — Grapes, dates, apples, oranges
- Roots and tubers — Potatoes
- Pulses — Broad and horse beans
- Others — Nuts, cocoa beans

IRRIGATION

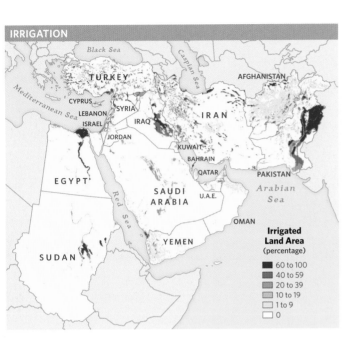

Irrigated
Land Area
(percentage)

- 60 to 100
- 40 to 59
- 20 to 39
- 10 to 19
- 1 to 9
- 0

These center pivot-irrigated alfalfa fields in south-central Saudi Arabia are utilizing fossil water — a non-renewable water source that is trapped deep below the surface. In many areas of the arid Middle East, where water use is dominated by irrigation, total water usage exceeds current recharge rates — dooming the long-term future of irrigation in those areas.

NET TRADE IN FOOD

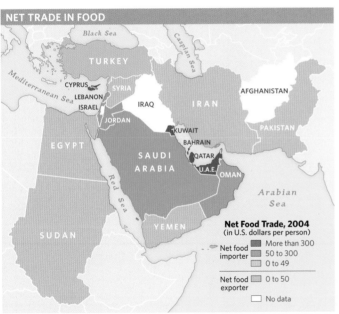

Net Food Trade, 2004
(in U.S. dollars per person)

Net food importer
- More than 300
- 50 to 300
- 0 to 49

Net food exporter
- 0 to 50

- No data

PRODUCTION BY COMMODITY GROUP

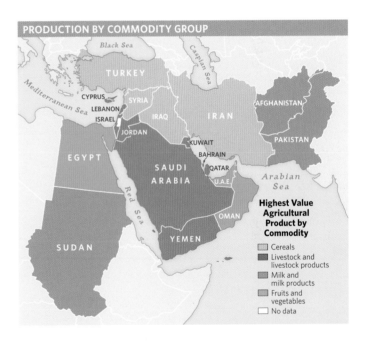

Highest Value
Agricultural
Product by
Commodity

- Cereals
- Livestock and livestock products
- Milk and milk products
- Fruits and vegetables
- No data

AGRICULTURAL PRODUCTION OVER TIME

Countries included: Cyprus, Egypt, Iran, Israel, Jordan, Kuwait, Lebanon, Pakistan, Saudi Arabia, Sudan, Syria, Turkey, United Arab Emirates, Yemen

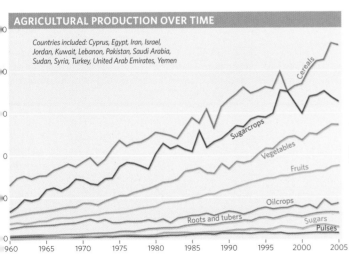

Cereals, Sugarcrops, Vegetables, Fruits, Oilcrops, Roots and tubers, Sugars, Pulses

1960 1965 1970 1975 1980 1985 1990 1995 2000 2005

FISH PRODUCTION OVER TIME

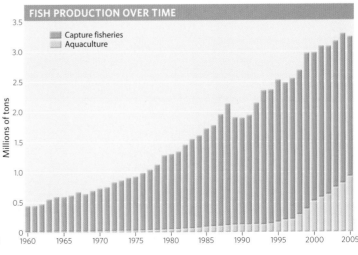

- Capture fisheries
- Aquaculture

Millions of tons

3.5 3.0 2.5 2.0 1.5 1.0 0.5 0

1960 1965 1970 1975 1980 1985 1990 1995 2000 2005

Development Indicators

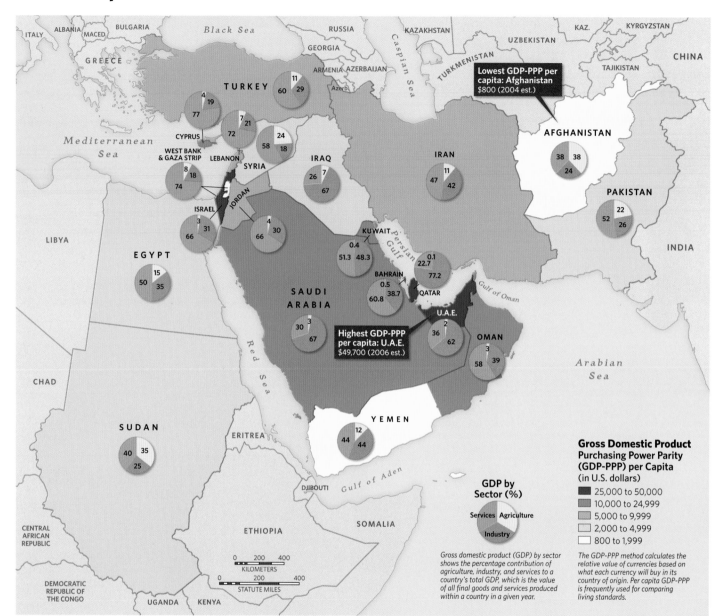

Lowest GDP-PPP per capita: Afghanistan $800 (2004 est.)

Highest GDP-PPP per capita: U.A.E. $49,700 (2006 est.)

Gross Domestic Product
Purchasing Power Parity (GDP-PPP) per Capita
(in U.S. dollars)

- 25,000 to 50,000
- 10,000 to 24,999
- 5,000 to 9,999
- 2,000 to 4,999
- 800 to 1,999

The GDP-PPP method calculates the relative value of currencies based on what each currency will buy in its country of origin. Per capita GDP-PPP is frequently used for comparing living standards.

GDP by Sector (%)

Services Agriculture Industry

Gross domestic product (GDP) by sector shows the percentage contribution of agriculture, industry, and services to a country's total GDP, which is the value of all final goods and services produced within a country in a given year.

KILOMETERS 0 200 400
STATUTE MILES 0 200 400

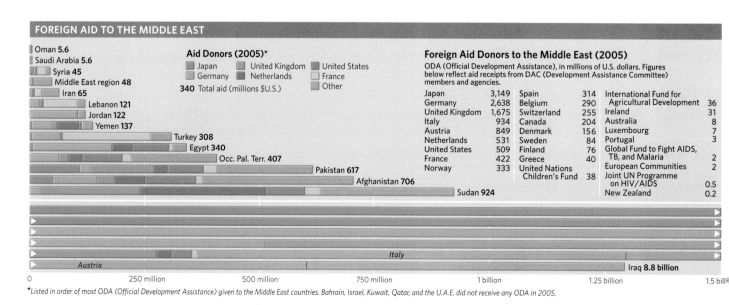

FOREIGN AID TO THE MIDDLE EAST

- Oman **5.6**
- Saudi Arabia **5.6**
- Syria **45**
- Middle East region **48**
- Iran **65**
- Lebanon **121**
- Jordan **122**
- Yemen **137**
- Turkey **308**
- Egypt **340**
- Occ. Pal. Terr. **407**
- Pakistan **617**
- Afghanistan **706**
- Sudan **924**

Austria
Italy
Iraq **8.8 billion**

Aid Donors (2005)*
- Japan
- Germany
- United Kingdom
- Netherlands
- United States
- France
- Other

340 Total aid (millions $U.S.)

Foreign Aid Donors to the Middle East (2005)
ODA (Official Development Assistance), in millions of U.S. dollars. Figures below reflect aid receipts from DAC (Development Assistance Committee) members and agencies.

Japan	3,149	Spain	314	International Fund for Agricultural Development 36
Germany	2,638	Belgium	290	Ireland 31
United Kingdom	1,675	Switzerland	255	Australia 8
Italy	934	Canada	204	Luxembourg 7
Austria	849	Denmark	156	Portugal 3
Netherlands	531	Sweden	84	Global Fund to Fight AIDS, TB, and Malaria 2
United States	509	Finland	76	European Communities 2
France	422	Greece	40	Joint UN Programme on HIV/AIDS 0.5
Norway	333	United Nations Children's Fund	38	New Zealand 0.2

0   250 million   500 million   750 million   1 billion   1.25 billion   1.5 bill

*Listed in order of most ODA (Official Development Assistance) given to the Middle East countries. Bahrain, Israel, Kuwait, Qatar, and the U.A.E. did not receive any ODA in 2005.

MERCHANDISE IMPORTS

2005 figures, in billions of U.S. dollars.

Turkey	116.6	Qatar	10.1
U.A.E.	80.7	Lebanon	9.6
Saudi Arabia	59.4	Oman	9.0
Israel	47.1	Syria	8.1
Iran	35.9	Bahrain	7.7
Pakistan	25.3	Sudan	6.8
Iraq	23.4	Cyprus	6.3
Egypt	19.8	Yemen	4.3
Kuwait	16.3	Afghanistan	3.2
Jordan	10.5		

Merchandise includes fuels (petroleum, coal, gas, electric current), minerals, metals, chemicals, machinery, office and telecom equipment, agricultural products, textiles, clothing and other manufactures.

MERCHANDISE EXPORTS

2005 figures, in billions of U.S. dollars.

Saudi Arabia	181.4	Egypt	10.7
U.A.E.	115.5	Bahrain	9.9
Turkey	73.4	Yemen	6.4
Iran	56.3	Syria	5.8
Kuwait	45.0	Sudan	4.8
Israel	42.7	Jordan	4.3
Qatar	25.8	Lebanon	2.3
Iraq	24.1	Cyprus	1.5
Oman	18.7	Afghanistan	0.6
Pakistan	15.9		

SCHOOL ENROLLMENT

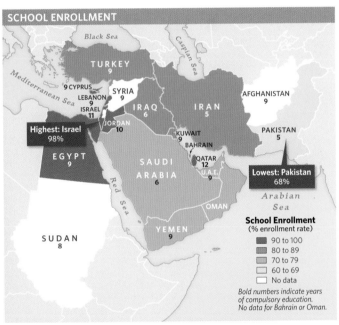

Highest: Israel 98%

Lowest: Pakistan 68%

School Enrollment
(% enrollment rate)
- 90 to 100
- 80 to 89
- 70 to 79
- 60 to 69
- No data

Bold numbers indicate years of compulsory education. No data for Bahrain or Oman.

LITERACY RATES

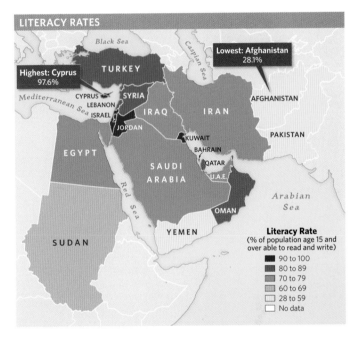

Highest: Cyprus 97.6%

Lowest: Afghanistan 28.1%

Literacy Rate
(% of population age 15 and over able to read and write)
- 90 to 100
- 80 to 89
- 70 to 79
- 60 to 69
- 28 to 59
- No data

INFANT MORTALITY

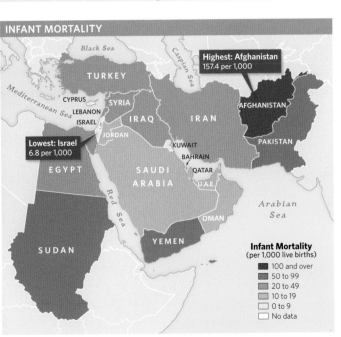

Highest: Afghanistan 157.4 per 1,000

Lowest: Israel 6.8 per 1,000

Infant Mortality
(per 1,000 live births)
- 100 and over
- 50 to 99
- 20 to 49
- 10 to 19
- 0 to 9
- No data

ACCESS TO SANITATION SERVICES

Highest, 100%: Bahrain, Cyprus, Israel, Qatar and Saudi Arabia

Lowest, 34%: Afghanistan and Sudan

Access to Sanitation
(% of total population)
- 90 to 100
- 80 to 89
- 70 to 79
- 50 to 69
- 24 to 49
- No data

World Heritage Sites

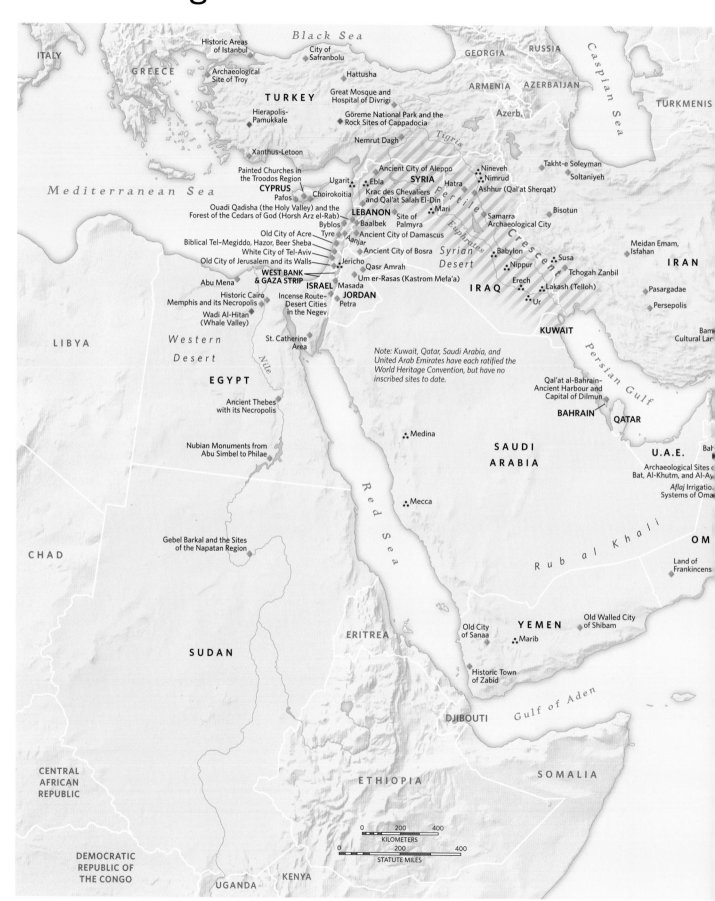

Black Sea

ITALY

GREECE

TURKEY

Historic Areas
of Istanbul

City of
Safranbolu

Archaeological
Site of Troy

Hattusha

Great Mosque and
Hospital of Divrigi

Hierapolis-
Pamukkale

Göreme National Park and the
Rock Sites of Cappadocia

Nemrut Dagh

Xanthus-Letoon

Painted Churches in
the Troodos Region

CYPRUS

Pafos

Ugarit

Choirokoitia

Ancient City of Aleppo

Ebla

SYRIA

Krac des Chevaliers
and Qal'at Salah El-Din

Ouadi Qadisha (the Holy Valley) and the
Forest of the Cedars of God (Horsh Arz el-Rab)

LEBANON

Byblos

Baalbek

Site of
Palmyra

Old City of Acre

Tyre

Aanjar

Ancient City of Damascus

Biblical Tel-Megiddo, Hazor, Beer Sheba

White City of Tel-Aviv

Ancient City of Bosra

Old City of Jerusalem and its Walls

Jericho

Qasr Amrah

WEST BANK
& GAZA STRIP

Um er-Rasas (Kastrom Mefa'a)

Abu Mena

ISRAEL

Masada

Historic Cairo

JORDAN

Memphis and its Necropolis

Petra

Incense Route–
Desert Cities
in the Negev

Wadi Al-Hitan
(Whale Valley)

LIBYA

Western
Desert

St. Catherine
Area

EGYPT

Ancient Thebes
with its Necropolis

Nubian Monuments from
Abu Simbel to Philae

CHAD

Gebel Barkal and the Sites
of the Napatan Region

CENTRAL
AFRICAN
REPUBLIC

DEMOCRATIC
REPUBLIC OF
THE CONGO

SUDAN

ERITREA

Mediterranean Sea

Nineveh

Nimrud

Hatra

Ashhur (Qal'at Sherqat)

Mari

Samarra
Archaeological City

Babylon

Nippur

Erech

Ur

Lakash (Telloh)

IRAQ

Takht-e Soleyman

Soltaniyeh

Bisotun

Meidan Emam,
Isfahan

IRAN

Susa

Tchogah Zanbil

Pasargadae

Persepolis

Fertile Crescent

Tigris

Euphrates

Syrian
Desert

GEORGIA

RUSSIA

ARMENIA

AZERBAIJAN

Azerb.

Caspian Sea

TURKMENIS

KUWAIT

Persian Gulf

Note: Kuwait, Qatar, Saudi Arabia, and
United Arab Emirates have each ratified the
World Heritage Convention, but have no
inscribed sites to date.

Qal'at al-Bahrain-
Ancient Harbour and
Capital of Dilmun

BAHRAIN

QATAR

U.A.E.

Bam
Cultural Lar

Bah

Archaeological Sites c
Bat, Al-Khutm, and Al-Ay.

Aflaj Irrigatio.
Systems of Oma

Nile

Red Sea

Medina

Mecca

SAUDI
ARABIA

Rub al Khali

OM

Land of
Frankincens

Old City
of Sanaa

YEMEN

Marib

Old Walled City
of Shibam

Historic Town
of Zabid

DJIBOUTI

Gulf of Aden

ETHIOPIA

SOMALIA

UGANDA

KENYA

0 200 400
KILOMETERS

0 200 400
STATUTE MILES

Ancient Egypt

Cultural Landscape and
Archaeological Remains
of the Bamian Valley

Buddhist Ruins of Takht-i-Bahi
and Neighboring City Remains
at Sahr-i-Bahlol

UZBEKISTAN

CHINA

TAJIKISTAN

Taxila

Minaret and Archaeological
Remains of Jam

Rohtas
Fort

AFGHANISTAN

Fort and Shalamar
Gardens in Lahore

PAKISTAN

Archaeological Ruins
at Mohenjo Daro

INDIA

Historical
Monuments
of Thatta

Gulf of
Oman

Arabian
Sea

World Heritage Sites

The World Heritage List was established
under the terms of the 1972 UNESCO
"Convention Concerning the Protection of
the World Cultural and Natural Heritage."
Its purpose is to encourage the identification,
protection, and preservation of cultural and
natural heritage around the world considered
to be of outstanding value to humanity.

◆ Cultural heritage site

Cultural heritage refers to monuments,
groups of buildings, and sites with historical,
aesthetic, archaeological, scientific,
ethnological, or anthropological value.

◆ Natural heritage site

Natural heritage refers to outstanding
physical, biological, and geological formations;
habitats of threatened species of animals and
plants; and areas with scientific, conservation,
or aesthetic value.

◆ Mixed site

Mixed sites are sites with both
cultural and natural values.

▨ Fertile Crescent

⸭ Other selected site of
historical/archaeological interest
(not on World Heritage List)

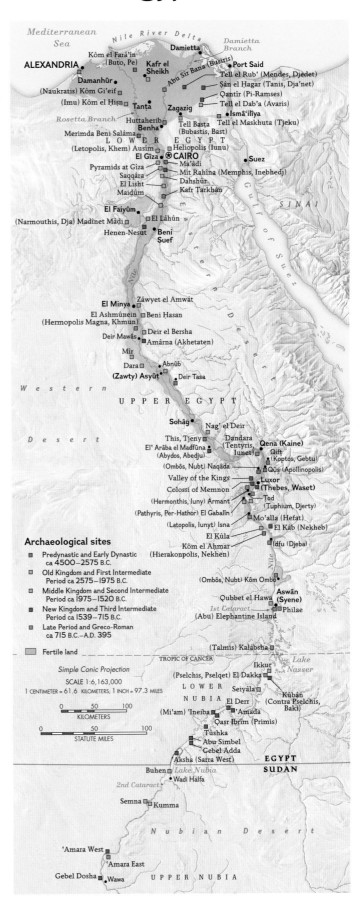

Mediterranean
Sea

Nile River Delta

Damietta
Branch

Kôm el Farâ'în
(Buto, Pe)

Damietta

ALEXANDRIA

Kafr el
Sheikh

Abu Sîr Bana (Busiris)

Port Said

Tell el Rub' (Mendes, Djedet)

Damanhûr

Sân el Hagar (Tanis, Dja'net)

(Naukratis) Kôm Gi'eif

Qantîr (Pi-Ramses)

(Imu) Kôm el Hisn

Tanta

Zagazig

Tell el Dab'a (Avaris)

Ismâ'ilîya

Rosetta Branch

Huttaherib

Tell el Maskhuta (Tjeku)

Merimda Beni Salâma

Benha

Tell Basta
(Bubastis, Bast)

(Letopolis, Khem) Ausim

Heliopolis (Iunu)

LOWER EGYPT

El Gîza

CAIRO

Pyramids at Giza

Ma'âdi

Saqqâra

Mit Rahîna (Memphis, Inebhedj)

El Lisht

Dahshûr

Maidûm

Kafr Tarkhân

Suez

SINAI

El Faiyûm

El Lâhûn

(Narmouthis, Dja) Madînet Mâdi

Henen-Nesut

Beni
Suef

Gulf of Suez

El Minya

Zâwyet el Amwât

El Ashmûnein
(Hermopolis Magna, Khmun)

Beni Hasan

Deir Mawâs

Deir el Bersha

Amârna (Akhetaten)

Mîr

Dara

Abnûb

(Zawty) Asyût

Deir Tasa

Western

UPPER EGYPT

Desert

Sohâg

Nag' el Deir

This, Tjeny

Dandara
(Tentyris,
Iunet)

Qena (Kaine)

El' Arâba el Madfûna
(Abydos, Abedju)

Qift
(Koptos, Gebtu)

(Ombôs, Nubt) Naqâda

Qûs (Apollinopolis)

Valley of the Kings

Luxor

Colossi of Memnon

(Thebes, Waset)

(Hermonthis, Iuny) Armant

Tod
(Tuphium, Djerty)

(Pathyris, Per-Hathor) El Gabalîn

Mo'alla (Hefat)

(Latopolis, Iunyt) Isna

El Kâb (Nekheb)

El Kûla

Idfu (Djeba)

Kôm el Ahmar (Hierakonpolis, Nekhen)

Archaeological sites

▪ Predynastic and Early Dynastic
ca 4500–2575 B.C.

▫ Old Kingdom and First Intermediate
Period ca 2575–1975 B.C.

▫ Middle Kingdom and Second Intermediate
Period ca 1975–1520 B.C.

▪ New Kingdom and Third Intermediate
Period ca 1539–715 B.C.

▫ Late Period and Greco-Roman
ca 715 B.C.–A.D. 395

▨ Fertile land

(Ombôs, Nubt) Kôm Ombo

Qubbet el Hawa

Aswân
(Syene)

1st Cataract

Philae

(Abu) Elephantine Island

(Talmis) Kalâbsha

TROPIC OF CANCER

Lake
Nasser

Ikkur

(Pselchis, Pselqet) El Dakka

LOWER

Seiyâla

Kûbân
(Contra Pselchis,
Baki)

NUBIA

El Derr

(Mi'am) 'Ineiba

'Amada

Qasr Ibrîm (Primis)

Tûshka

Abu Simbel

Gebel Adda

Aksha (Sarra West)

EGYPT

SUDAN

Buhen

Lake Nubia

Wadi Halfa

2nd Cataract

Semna

Kumma

Nubian Desert

'Amara West

'Amara East

Gebel Dosha

Wawa

UPPER NUBIA

Simple Conic Projection

SCALE 1:6,163,000

1 CENTIMETER = 61.6 KILOMETERS; 1 INCH = 97.3 MILES

0   50   100
KILOMETERS

0   50   100
STATUTE MILES

Suez Canal

Below sea level

Navigation channel

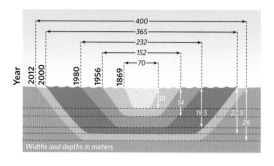

Widths and depths in meters

Periodic Widening of the Canal

Spurred on by increasing ship sizes and other tech-nological developments, the canal has been widened several times over its history. Plans are in place to fur-ther deepen it by 2012, which will make it possible for fully-loaded supertankers to pass through. There is also a height limit of 68 meters, the space required to pass under the Suez Canal Bridge at El Qantara. Unlike the Panama Canal the terrain is flat, and there are no locks.

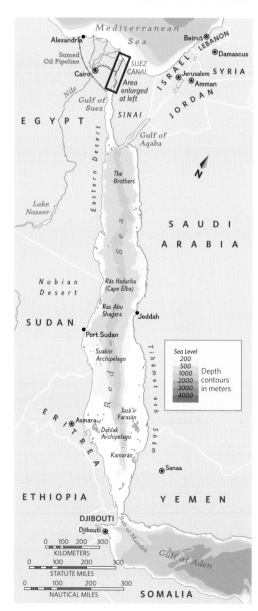

Depth contours in meters

The Canal's Beginnings

The first known formal survey for the purpose of building a waterway along the canal's current route was completed under the authority of Napoleon Bonaparte. However, the project was deemed too complicated and expensive at the time and thus abandoned. Following more favorable subsequent studies, the idea was revisited by a French diplomat named Ferdinand de Lesseps. With permis-sion from the Ottoman Viceroy of Egypt, the Suez Canal Company was formed, with funding mainly from French small investors along with the then-ruler of Egypt. Construction began in 1859 and took almost 11 years, completed partly by as many as 30,000 Egyptian forced laborers—many of whom lost their lives.

1869–1956

The canal officially opened on November 17th, 1869, and it had a dramatic and lasting impact on the dynamics of world trade. In 1875 the Egyptian leader, beset with financial difficulties, was forced to sell his country's shares, which were imme-diately purchased by the British gov-ernment. For Britain, the canal held great strategic value, as it offered a seaborne shortcut to its most impor-tant possession, India. During the late 1800s and early 1900s, Britain ben-efited perhaps more than any other country from the canal, having also used it to its advantage by controlling ships' passage during World Wars I and II. British troops remained until 1956, leaving then under the terms of an agreement with Egypt.

1957 to Present

In 1957, after a multinational dispute which led to its closure for several months, the canal reopened under Egyptian control. Ten years later it was again closed (due to blockage by sunken ships during the Arab-Israeli War), and not reopened until 1975. It has been operated by the Egyptian government's Suez Canal Authority ever since. For the past several decades, oil has no longer accounted for the majority of shipments, due to the increasing size of tankers that are too big for the canal. Many tankers send their oil via the Sumed (Suez-Mediterranean) Pipeline, bypassing the canal. More recently, the amount of container ship activity has grown significantly, now making up the larg-est share of traffic through the canal.

See the flag of the Suez Canal on pages 112–113, Flags of the Middle East

Regional History

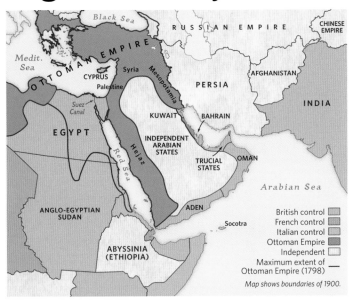

Map shows boundaries of 1900.

British control
French control
Italian control
Ottoman Empire
Independent
Maximum extent of Ottoman Empire (1798)

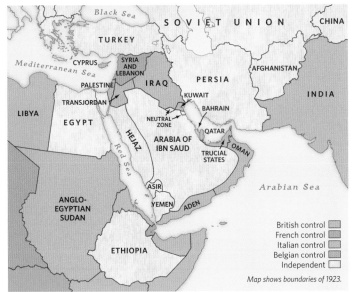

Map shows boundaries of 1923.

British control
French control
Italian control
Belgian control
Independent

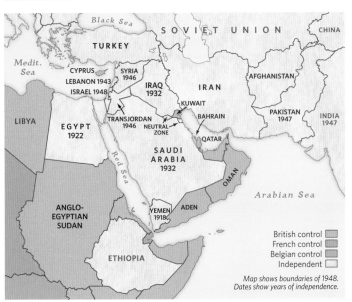

Map shows boundaries of 1948. Dates show years of independence.

British control
French control
Belgian control
Independent

1900: Chain of Alliances

By 1900, the former dominance of the Ottoman Empire was on the decline, with European countries (including France, Britain, and Italy) gradually gaining control of former Ottoman territories in parts of Arabia and Northern Africa. Britain in particular had established a strong foothold in the region. Motivated in part by a desire to guarantee safe passage through the Suez Canal and Red Sea for voyages to and from India, Britain seized de facto control of Egypt in 1882. Around this time the British also established treaties with the small sheikdoms of the Arabian Peninsula, effectively stringing a chain of alliances that would help uphold their interests in southern Asia and the Middle East.

1923: European Imperialism

With the collapse of the Ottoman Empire following World War I, occupying European powers carved up the region under a mandate system established by the newly-formed League of Nations. In one example, it authorized Britain (in 1920) to set up a postwar government in Iraq. Britain drew the new country's boundaries according to its own strategic needs, largely around old Ottoman provinces. The foreign presence rallied the Iraqis and awakened a sense of nationalism that would eventually drive the British from Iraq. Similarly, many other recent and current conflicts in the Middle East can be at least partly attributed to the drawing of administrative boundaries by European powers.

1948: Rise of Nationalism

Encouraged by the British during World War I as a weapon against the Ottomans, Arab nationalism continued to grow during the decades-long presence of European powers in the Middle East. Revolts in Egypt had forced Britain to grant it limited independence in 1922. Following World War II, Zionists pushed for creation of a Jewish homeland and poured into Palestine, causing friction with Palestinian Arabs. The British Mandate of Palestine was divided into separate Arab and Jewish parts, and when the British withdrew in 1948, Israel declared itself a state. By then, nationalist movements had achieved independence for Syria and Lebanon (from France), as well as Iraq and Jordan (from Britain).

Ottoman Sultan Ghazi Mehmed Rechad V, pictured circa 1917, reigned from 1909 until his death in 1918. For roughly 500 years, the Ottoman Empire controlled the crossroads of three continents, finally dissolving in 1922 in the aftermath of World War I.

British General Edmund Allenby, commander of British forces in Palestine, enters Jerusalem's Jaffa Gate on foot, out of respect for the holy city, on December 11, 1917. Led by Allenby, the British army had captured the city from Ottoman forces two days earlier. The capture of Jerusalem, along with the military successes of Lieutenant-Colonel T.E. Lawrence, or "Lawrence of Arabia," was instrumental in Britain's efforts to defeat the Ottomans during World War I.

Regional Conflicts

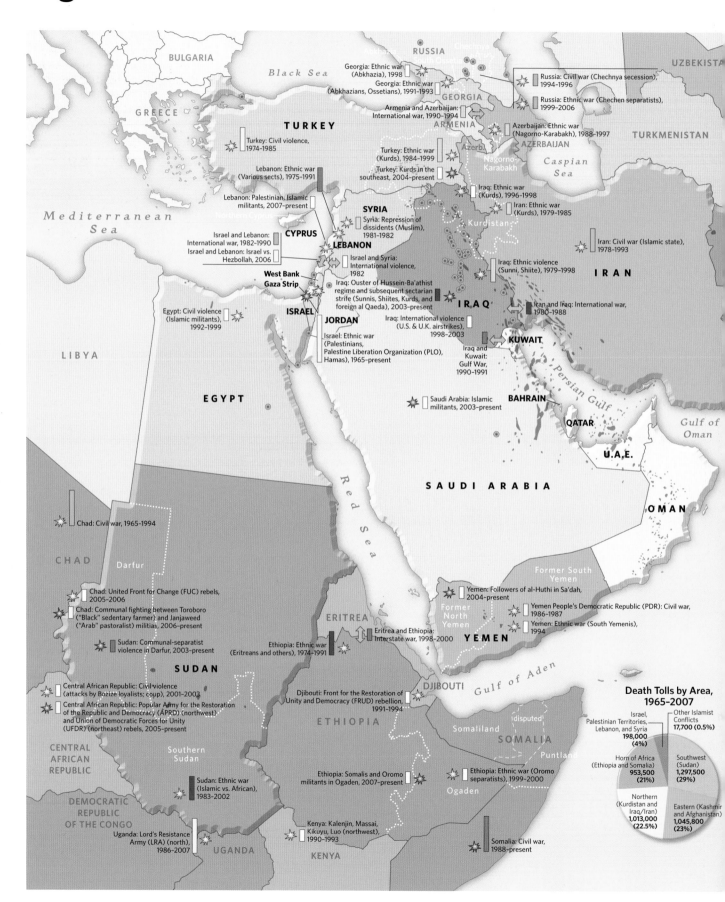

BULGARIA

Black Sea

GREECE

Mediterranean
Sea

RUSSIA

Georgia: Ethnic war
(Abkhazia), 1998

Georgia: Ethnic war
(Abkhazians, Ossetians), 1991-1993

GEORGIA

Armenia and Azerbaijan:
International war, 1990-1994

ARMENIA

Azerb.

AZERBAIJAN

Russia: Civil war (Chechnya secession),
1994-1996

Russia: Ethnic war (Chechen separatists),
1999-2006

Azerbaijan: Ethnic war
(Nagorno-Karabakh), 1988-1997

Nagorno-
Karabakh

Caspian
Sea

UZBEKISTA

TURKMENISTAN

TURKEY

Turkey: Civil violence,
1974-1985

Lebanon: Ethnic war
(Various sects), 1975-1991

Lebanon: Palestinian, Islamic
militants, 2007-present

Israel and Lebanon:
International war, 1982-1990

Israel and Lebanon: Israel vs.
Hezbollah, 2006

West Bank
Gaza Strip

Egypt: Civil violence
(Islamic militants),
1992-1999

ISRAEL

JORDAN

Israel: Ethnic war
(Palestinians,
Palestine Liberation Organization (PLO),
Hamas), 1965-present

CYPRUS

Northern Cyprus

LEBANON

SYRIA

Syria: Repression of
dissidents (Muslim),
1981-1982

Turkey: Ethnic war
(Kurds), 1984-1999

Turkey: Kurds in the
southeast, 2004-present

Israel and Syria:
International violence,
1982

Iraq: Ouster of Hussein-Ba'athist
regime and subsequent sectarian
strife (Sunnis, Shiites, Kurds, and
foreign al Qaeda), 2003-present

Iraq: International violence
(U.S. & U.K. airstrikes),
1998-2003

IRAQ

Iraq: Ethnic war
(Kurds), 1996-1998

Iran: Ethnic war
(Kurds), 1979-1985

Kurdistan

Iraq: Ethnic violence
(Sunni, Shiite), 1979-1998

Iran and Iraq: International war,
1980-1988

KUWAIT

Iraq and
Kuwait:
Gulf War,
1990-1991

Iran: Civil war (Islamic state),
1978-1993

IRAN

LIBYA

EGYPT

Saudi Arabia: Islamic
militants, 2003-present

BAHRAIN

QATAR

U.A.E.

Persian Gulf

Gulf of
Oman

SAUDI ARABIA

OMAN

Red Sea

Chad: Civil war, 1965-1994

CHAD

Darfur

Chad: United Front for Change (FUC) rebels,
2005-2006

Chad: Communal fighting between Toroboro
("Black" sedentary farmer) and Janjaweed
("Arab" pastoralist) militias, 2006-present

Sudan: Communal-separatist
violence in Darfur, 2003-present

SUDAN

Central African Republic: Civil violence
(attacks by Bozize loyalists; coup), 2001-2003

Central African Republic: Popular Army for the Restoration
of the Republic and Democracy (APRD) (northwest)
and Union of Democratic Forces for Unity
(UFDR) (northeast) rebels, 2005-present

CENTRAL
AFRICAN
REPUBLIC

Southern
Sudan

Sudan: Ethnic war
(Islamic vs. African),
1983-2002

DEMOCRATIC
REPUBLIC
OF THE CONGO

Uganda: Lord's Resistance
Army (LRA) (north),
1986-2007

UGANDA

ERITREA

Eritrea and Ethiopia:
Interstate war, 1998-2000

Ethiopia: Ethnic war
(Eritreans and others), 1974-1991

Former
North
Yemen

Former South
Yemen

Yemen: Followers of al-Huthi in Sa'dah,
2004-present

Yemen People's Democratic Republic (PDR): Civil war,
1986-1987

Yemen: Ethnic war (South Yemenis),
1994

YEMEN

Gulf of Aden

DJIBOUTI

Djibouti: Front for the Restoration of
Unity and Democracy (FRUD) rebellion,
1991-1994

ETHIOPIA

Ethiopia: Somalis and Oromo
militants in Ogaden, 2007-present

Ethiopia: Ethnic war (Oromo
separatists), 1999-2000

Ogaden

Somaliland

SOMALIA

Puntland

disputed

Kenya: Kalenjin, Massai,
Kikuyu, Luo (northwest),
1990-1993

KENYA

Somalia: Civil war,
1988-present

Death Tolls by Area,
1965-2007

Israel,
Palestinian Territories,
Lebanon, and Syria
198,000
(4%)

Other Islamist
Conflicts
17,700 (0.5%)

Horn of Africa
(Ethiopia and Somalia)
953,500
(21%)

Southwest
(Sudan)
1,297,500
(29%)

Northern
(Kurdistan and
Iraq/Iran)
1,013,000
(22.5%)

Eastern (Kashmir
and Afghanistan)
1,045,800
(23%)

Regional Regime Types

Although there has been a dramatic increase in the number of democratic regimes in the world since the mid-1980s, there are few democratic regimes in the Middle East, and even these regimes have serious divisions. Democratic experiments have often been thwarted by the fear of Islamist parties gaining control. Several autocratic regimes have been replaced by "mixed authority" ones: regimes in Iraq and Afghanistan are supported by Western forces and the others are split by contenders for power. Six of the world's few remaining monarchies are found here, controlling the region's "oil emirates." Three other autocracies struggle to control internal challenges.

Regional Warfare Trends

The Middle East, like other regions of the world, experienced a dramatic increase in internal (societal) wars during the Cold War era, as external powers' competition for influence exacerbated internal tensions. The region was unique in the number of serious interstate wars that occurred there, involving rivalries between Arab States and Israel, Iraq and Iran, and Pakistan and India. Both societal and interstate warfare declined dramatically beginning in the mid-1980s; however, violent conflict has risen once again in the early 21st century as radical Islamist groups have initiated what they hope is a new revolution for control of this oil-rich region.

Weapons Possessions

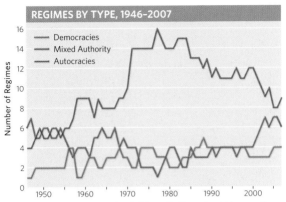

REGIMES BY TYPE, 1946–2007

Democracies score +6 to +10 on the Polity scale * (Cyprus, Israel, Lebanon, and Turkey in 2007); *Mixed Authority* regimes have middling Polity scores or occupational forces (Afghanistan, Egypt, Iraq, Jordan, Sudan, and Yemen in 2007); *Autocracies* score -10 to -6 on the Polity scale (Bahrain, Iran, Kuwait, Oman, Qatar, Pakistan, Saudi Arabia, Syria, and United Arab Emirates in 2007).

*The Polity scale is a widely used measure of democracy based on regime and authority characteristics.

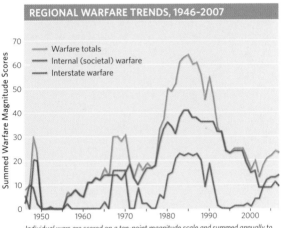

REGIONAL WARFARE TRENDS, 1946–2007

Individual wars are scored on a ten-point magnitude scale and summed annually to chart warfare trends over time. List of countries included: Afghanistan, Bahrain, Cyprus, Egypt, Iran, Iraq, Israel, Jordan, Kuwait, Lebanon, Oman, Pakistan, Qatar, Saudi Arabia, Sudan, Syria, Turkey, United Arab Emirates, and Yemen.

Regional Conflicts and State Fragility

States and political regions are complex social systems that combine, organize, and coordinate essential functions and services to sustain, and improve, the quality of life for their inhabitants. These include both legitimacy and effectiveness in the provision of four essential functions: security, governance, economics and trade, and social services. The "State Fragility Index" assesses state performance deficits in these essential functions and provides a general measure of the country's current and future prospects, including its ability to govern and manage political conflict. Violent conflict is both a major cause and consequence of state fragility. The Middle East is a region of contrasts in terms of state fragility and conflict, especially when it is considered in the broader context of Muslim countries. The oil-rich countries of the Arabian Peninsula remain largely isolated and relatively secure, whereas the oil-producing states of Iraq and Iran are immersed in regional tensions and have grown more violent and fragile as a result. Sudan, especially, is both extremely violent and fragile and is surrounded by extremely fragile and violent states. External assistance has lessened fragility in Egypt, Israel, and Pakistan but external intervention has increased fragility in Iraq and Afghanistan. Oil competition, state fragility, and violent conflict combine to create a volatile mix in this region.

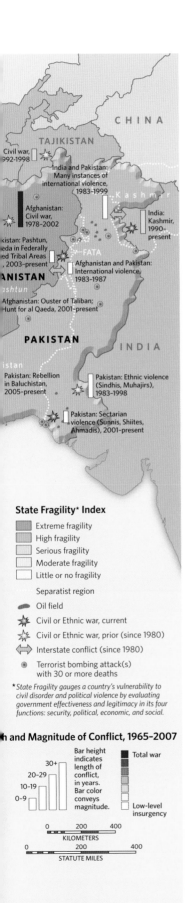

CHINA

TAJIKISTAN

Civil war, 992-1998

India and Pakistan: Many instances of international violence, 1983-1999

Kashmir

Afghanistan: Civil war, 1978-2002

India: Kashmir, 1990-present

kistan: Pashtun, eda in Federally ed Tribal Areas , 2003-present

FATA

Afghanistan and Pakistan: International violence, 1983-1987

ANISTAN

ashtun

Afghanistan: Ouster of Taliban; Hunt for al Qaeda, 2001-present

PAKISTAN   INDIA

stan

Pakistan: Rebellion in Baluchistan, 2005-present

Pakistan: Ethnic violence (Sindhis, Muhajirs), 1983-1998

Pakistan: Sectarian violence (Sunnis, Shiites, Ahmadis), 2001-present

State Fragility* Index

- Extreme fragility
- High fragility
- Serious fragility
- Moderate fragility
- Little or no fragility
- Separatist region
- Oil field
- Civil or Ethnic war, current
- Civil or Ethnic war, prior (since 1980)
- Interstate conflict (since 1980)
- Terrorist bombing attack(s) with 30 or more deaths

*State Fragility gauges a country's vulnerability to civil disorder and political violence by evaluating government effectiveness and legitimacy in its four functions: security, political, economic, and social.

h and Magnitude of Conflict, 1965-2007

Bar height indicates length of conflict, in years. Bar color conveys magnitude.

30+
20-29
10-19
0-9

Total war

Low-level insurgency

0   200   400
KILOMETERS

0   200   400
STATUTE MILES

	Nuclear		Chemical		Biological	
	Declared stockpile	Suspected or undeclared	Declared stockpile now being destroyed	Undeclared stockpile or development program	Suspected offensive development program	
Albania			●			
China	●			●	●	
Egypt				●	●	
France	●					
India	●		●		●	
Iran		●		●	●	
Israel	●			●	●	
Libya			●			
North Korea		●		●	●	
Pakistan	●					
Russia	●		●		●	
South Korea			●		●	
Syria				●	●	
U.K.	●					
U.S.	●		●		●	

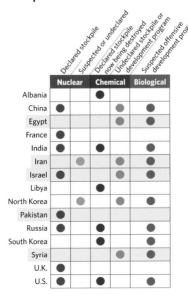

Israel and the Palestinians

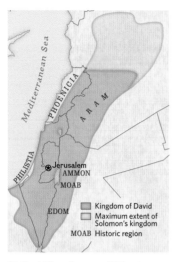

United Kingdom, ca 935 B.C.

According to the Bible, Joshua led the Israelites into lands west of the Jordan River, where they routed the Canaanites but failed to win Gaza from the Philistines. King David expanded Israel and moved his capital to the conquered Jebusite city of Jerusalem. There his son Solomon built the first Temple of the Lord.

Divided Kingdoms, ca 840 B.C.

Solomon's son Rehoboam was unable to prevent internal issues from dividing the kingdom of his forefathers. As Israel and Judah weakened, their sphere of influence diminished. Israel fell to the Assyrian Empire in 722 B.C. The Kingdom of Judah was finally conquered in 586 B.C. by Nebuchadnezzar of the Babylonian Empire. As each Hebrew kingdom collapsed many Jews were deported from their homeland.

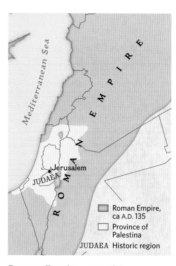

Roman Empire, A.D. 135

Rome administered this land as a provincial backwater, content to leave Judaea to the governance of local puppet monarchs. But when anti-Roman anger exploded in the Jewish Revolt of 66, the empire came down hard. Roman legions crushed the rebels, and some Jews were dispersed. After the Bar Kochba revolt in 132, Rome deported the remaining Jews, renaming the region Palestina, for the Philistine people who predated them.

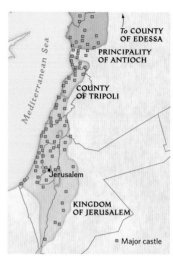

Crusader States, 1140

Launched to regain the Holy Land for Christians, the First Crusade besieged and conquered Jerusalem in 1099. Several Crusader states, which suffered constant attacks, were established in the Eastern Mediterranean. Once the Mamluks defeated their most imposing enemy (the Mongols) in 1260, they focused their Muslim army on the Crusader states, the last of which fell in 1291.

British Mandate, 1922–1948

As part of the settlement ending World War I, Britain governed Palestine with a League of Nations Mandate. Under the British, Jewish immigration steadily increased, alarming local Arabs. Riots and terrorism erupted as both sides lashed out at each other—and the British. As pressure mounted after World War II, Britain turned to the United Nations. This led to the U.N. Partition Plan.

Israel's Independence, 1948

When Britain withdrew in 1948, Israel declared its independence and five neighboring Arab governments mobilized for war. Well-led and better organized, Israel repulsed the Arab armies and seized more of Palestine than the UN plan had prescribed, uprooting 750,000 Palestinians. Jordan annexed Jerusalem's Old City and the West Bank, while Egypt occupied the Gaza Strip.

Six Day War, 1967

In early 1967 Egypt and Syria appeared to be readying an attack on Israel. On June 5, the Jewish state struck first, seizing the Sinai Peninsula and Gaza Strip. When Jordan attacked, Israel retaliated, capturing all of Jerusalem and the West Bank. Up north, Israel captured Syria's Golan Heights. The UN later passed a resolution calling for Israel to withdraw from occupied territory.

Yom Kippur War, 1973

On one of the most important Jewish holidays, Egypt and Syria launched a surprise attack against Israel, which soon countered and threatened to destroy Egyptian forces when a cease-fire was signed. There were Cold War implications, with the United States (for Israel) and the Soviet Union (for Egypt and Syria) providing arms assistance while jockeying for position in the Middle East.

Population

- Israeli settlements
- Palestinian towns
- ● ● More than 30,000
- ○ ○ 5,000–30,000
- · · Less than 5,000

Israeli Separation Barrier

—— Complete, 2007

----- Planned

0 5 10
KILOMETERS

0 5 10
STATUTE MILES

Israeli-Palestinian Diplomacy and Proposals

1937	Peel Commission
1947	United Nations Partition Plan
1949	Armistice Agreements
1967	Allon Plan
1970	Rogers Plan
1973	Geneva Conference
1978	Camp David Accords
1979	Israel-Egypt Peace Treaty
1991	Madrid Conference
1993	Oslo Accords
1994	Israel-Jordan Treaty of Peace
2000	Middle East Peace Summit at Camp David
2001	Taba Summit
2002	The Israeli Initiative (Elon Peace Plan)
2003	Road Map for Peace
2003	Geneva Accord
2005	Sharm el Sheikh Summit
2007	Annapolis Conference

March 1979: Egyptian President Anwar Sadat, left, U.S. President Jimmy Carter, center, and Israeli Prime Minister Menachem Begin clasp hands on the north lawn of the White House as they complete the signing of the peace treaty between Egypt and Israel.

September 1993: Israeli Prime Minister Yitzhak Rabin, left, and PLO Chairman Yasser Arafat, right, shake hands as U.S. President Bill Clinton presides over the ceremony marking the signing of the peace accord between Israel and the Palestinians on the White House lawn.

Still Inching Toward Peace

The path to Arab-Israeli peace had a major breakthrough with the 1979 Israel-Egypt peace treaty. Since then, however, numerous attempts to solve the lingering conflict (see list, above right) have made little progress, largely due to the reluctance of both sides to yield on three main factors: the status of East Jerusalem; the right of return for Palestinian refugees; and Israeli settlements in occupied territory. Setbacks along the way have also contributed to the slow progress of peace talks. Palestinians began the Second Intifada, or uprising, against Israel in 2000, so far resulting in 6,000 deaths on both sides. Israel removed all its settlements in the Gaza Strip in 2005, but has also been building a highly controversial separation barrier which snakes through the West Bank, dividing Palestinian populations. Despite these difficulties, an independent Palestinian state is largely seen by both sides as the best chance for peace.

November 2007: U.S. President George W. Bush, center, looks on as Israeli Prime Minister Ehud Olmert, left, and Palestinian National Authority President Mahmoud Abbas shake hands at the U.S. Naval Academy during the Annapolis Conference in Maryland.

Iraq

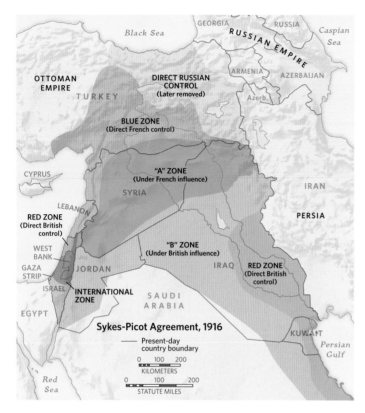

Sykes-Picot Agreement, 1916
— Present-day country boundary

0 100 200
KILOMETERS

0 100 200
STATUTE MILES

Persian, Arab, and Kurdish prisoners at a Mesopotamian prison camp in April 1916

Foreign Occupation in the Early 20th Century

Anticipating a victory over the Ottoman Empire in World War I, the British and French (with assent from Russia) forged the secret Sykes-Picot Agreement in 1916 to divide between themselves the Ottomans' vast holdings in the Middle East. This came despite promises made for national homelands for the Arabs, Kurds, Armenians, and other groups in return for their allegiance during the war. 1917 saw the Russian Revolution remove that country from the equa-

tion, but also the U.S. entry into the war. The U.S. was not keen on further European colonization in the Middle East. Although Sykes-Picot never materialized, widespread European occupation lasted until after World War II. Iraq received its independence from Britain in 1932, but British troops remained until 1958. European intent to dominate the region after World War I set a tone of discord between the West and many Middle Eastern groups—one that continues today.

U.S. launches air strikes against Iraq, 1991

Marines patrol Ramadi with night vision goggles and infrared lasers, 2007

Foreign Occupation Today

Following several decades as an independent republic, foreign occupation is again a reality for Iraq. After coalition forces had pushed Iraqi troops out of Kuwait in the 1991 Gulf War, the U.S. decided against an attempted occupation as the extra effort at the time would likely have fractured political alliances and cost unacceptable numbers of casualties. However, after the terrorist attacks of September 11, 2001, the world—in particular the United States—grew

more concerned about terrorism and weapons of mass destruction, which Iraq was believed to possess. In 2003, a U.S.-led coalition routed Iraqi forces in less than three weeks and occupied the country. Most Iraqis would like to see the coalition forces leave, but despite the creation of an Iraqi government, 164,000 coalition troops (154,000 of which are from the U.S.) were still in Iraq as of late 2007, training Iraqi police and struggling to keep the peace in parts of the country.

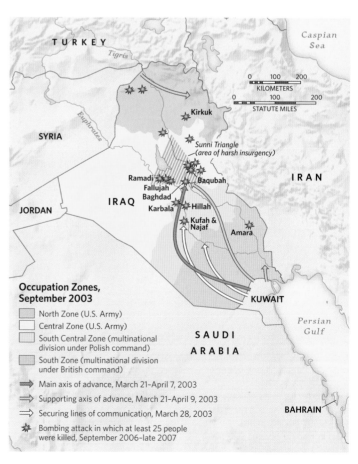

0 100 200
KILOMETERS

0 100 200
STATUTE MILES

Occupation Zones, September 2003

North Zone (U.S. Army)
Central Zone (U.S. Army)
South Central Zone (multinational division under Polish command)
South Zone (multinational division under British command)

⟹ Main axis of advance, March 21–April 7, 2003
⟹ Supporting axis of advance, March 21–April 9, 2003
⟹ Securing lines of communication, March 28, 2003
✻ Bombing attack in which at least 25 people were killed, September 2006–late 2007

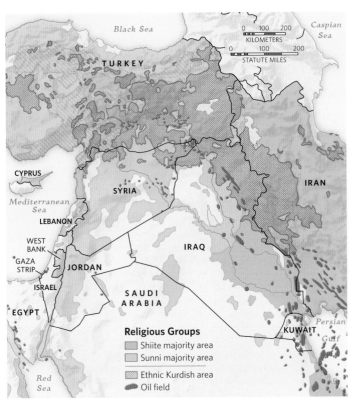

Sunni woman

Shiite woman

Kurdish woman

Religious Groups

☐ Shiite majority area
☐ Sunni majority area
▨ Ethnic Kurdish area
〰 Oil field

Internal Struggles

Iraq's initially foreign-imposed boundaries ignored local religious and ethnic groupings, and a geographic snapshot provides some insight into the struggles faced today. Internal competition for administrative control and oil fields is acting as a catalyst for much of the recent violence and animosity. Today some 4 million Iraqis, many of whom are skilled professionals, have been driven from their homes. Their absence only further exacerbates the difficulties of rebuilding the country's fragile infrastructure.

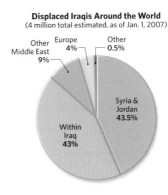

Displaced Iraqis Around the World
(4 million total estimated, as of Jan. 1, 2007)

Other Middle East 9%
Europe 4%
Other 0.5%
Syria & Jordan 43.5%
Within Iraq 43%

A car bombing in central Baghdad killed 81 people on February 12, 2007. Between 2003 and 2007, the total death toll from terrorist attacks in Baghdad exceeded 4,300.

Baghdad, Late 2007

Baghdad still hadn't fully recovered from the massive bombing campaign of the 1991 Gulf War when, on April 9, 2003, the city was occupied by U.S. ground forces as part of Operation Iraqi Freedom. The subsequent fall of Saddam Hussein's regime left a vacuum of control and security that allowed for rampant insurgent attacks against the occupying U.S. forces. With an effective government still eluding the city, the violence soon evolved into a power struggle,

largely between Sunnis and Shiites. The ongoing sectarian violence has taken many forms, including minority Sunnis bombing Shiite-controlled infrastructure (including sacred sites) with some Shiite groups exacting horrific revenge. In addition to fueling the flight of over 4 million Iraqis from their homes, the fear of random attacks has led to the near complete segregation of Baghdad's previously mixed neighborhoods into Sunni and Shiite strongholds (see map, right).

Neighborhoods of Baghdad (late 2007)

☐ Shiite majority
☐ Sunni majority
☐ Christians (of various sects and languages)
☐ Area in state of transition

PRIMARY SOURCE: *M.R. Izady (Sykes-Picot Agreement, 1916; Religious Groups; and Neighborhoods of Baghdad)*

Darfur

THE SITUATION IN DARFUR has become desperate for millions of displaced people, largely due to entire villages having been destroyed by Sudanese government forces and the Janjaweed, the government-supported militia. Drought and desertification had been stressing resources in the area for years, forcing Arab nomads and their livestock onto land farmed by Muslim African tribal groups. Oppressed by their own national government, rebel forces formed from the black African ethnic groups and began to fight. The Arab-controlled government soon went on a large-scale offensive, targeting and destroying hundreds of ethnic African villages—its henchmen guilty of murdering and raping civilians along the way. From this racially-charged conflict more than 2.5 million people have been uprooted. Some have flooded refugee camps over the border into Chad, but many more are trapped in countless camps within Darfur. Peace talks have been largely ineffective, partly due to the splintering of rebel group alliances. At first nearly oblivious to the crisis, the governments of the world have responded. In January 2008, a United Nations peacekeeping mission (UNAMID) took over for an overwhelmed African Union mission.

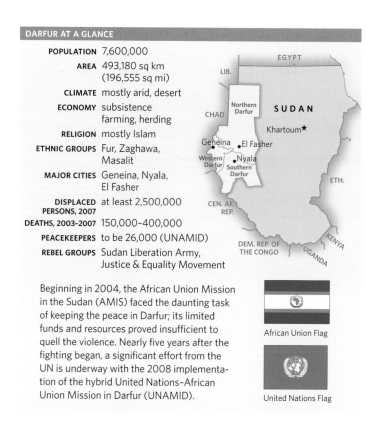

DARFUR AT A GLANCE

POPULATION	7,600,000
AREA	493,180 sq km (196,555 sq mi)
CLIMATE	mostly arid, desert
ECONOMY	subsistence farming, herding
RELIGION	mostly Islam
ETHNIC GROUPS	Fur, Zaghawa, Masalit
MAJOR CITIES	Geneina, Nyala, El Fasher
DISPLACED PERSONS, 2007	at least 2,500,000
DEATHS, 2003-2007	150,000–400,000
PEACEKEEPERS	to be 26,000 (UNAMID)
REBEL GROUPS	Sudan Liberation Army, Justice & Equality Movement

Beginning in 2004, the African Union Mission in the Sudan (AMIS) faced the daunting task of keeping the peace in Darfur; its limited funds and resources proved insufficient to quell the violence. Nearly five years after the fighting began, a significant effort from the UN is underway with the 2008 implementation of the hybrid United Nations–African Union Mission in Darfur (UNAMID).

African Union Flag

United Nations Flag

The village of Tama continues to burn more than a week after it was originally attacked by government-backed Arab militia in November 2005. The attackers continued to surround the village and would shoot at approaching vehicles. Since 2005 large-scale government attacks have declined, but millions of civilians remain displaced throughout the country.

Destruction of Villages

The practice of burning and pillaging the villages of ethnic Fur, Zaghawa, and Masalit people is a defining characteristic of the Darfur conflict. Hundreds of villages in the region have been documented as damaged or destroyed since 2003. The government-backed Janjaweed are infamous for their ruthless attacks on villages, with reports of murder, rape, and dismemberment of innocent women and children. In 2003, to counter rebel attacks against it, the Sudanese government adopted a strategy of attacking villages comprised of ethnic groups known to contribute members to the rebel groups. In some places, entire areas of ethnic African villages were wiped out, with Arab villages in those areas left untouched. Some damaged and destroyed villages have even been used and resettled by groups of Arab people. Unable to move back to their homes for fear of being attacked again, many people have been left with little choice but to move to crowded camps, where an uncertain future awaits them.

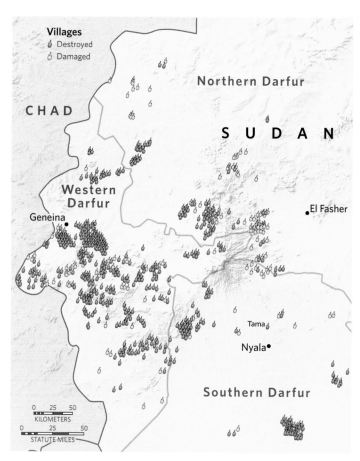

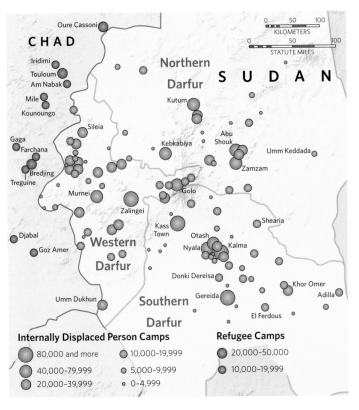

CHAD

Oure Cassoni

Iridimi
Touloum
Am Nabak
Mile
Kounoungo
Sileia
Gaga
Farchana
Bredjing
Treguine
Murnei
Zalingei
Djabal
Goz Amer

Western
Darfur

Umm Dukhun

0   50   100
KILOMETERS
0   50   100
STATUTE MILES

Northern
Darfur

S U D A N

Kutum
Kebkabiya
Abu Shouk
Golo
Kass Town
Otash
Nyala
Donki Dereisa
Gereida
El Ferdous

Southern
Darfur

Umm Keddada
Zamzam
Shearia
Kalma
Khor Omer
Adilla

Internally Displaced Person Camps
- 80,000 and more
- 40,000–79,999
- 20,000–39,999
- 10,000–19,999
- 5,000–9,999
- 0–4,999

Refugee Camps
- 20,000–50,000
- 10,000–19,999

Seeking Shelter

In order to escape the violence aimed at them, more than two million people have relocated to camps scattered across Darfur with another 230,000 having crossed the border into Chad to settle in refugee camps (map, left). Deaths in camps from disease and malnutrition were rampant at the height of the crisis in 2003–2004. Security in camps is a major concern, as even aid workers have been targeted and killed. Attacks on camps and humanitarian aid shipments further complicate the difficulty of getting help to people with little but the few possessions they could carry with them as they fled.

A woman carries her child in Abu Shouk camp in Northern Darfur (right), where more than 54,000 internally displaced people are seeking shelter. People from the Fur, Zaghawa, and Masalit ethnic groups have been the main targets of Sudanese government-sponsored attacks, fueling widespread cries of genocide from the international community.

An African Union peacekeeper guards a UN aid shipment in Geneina, Western Darfur.

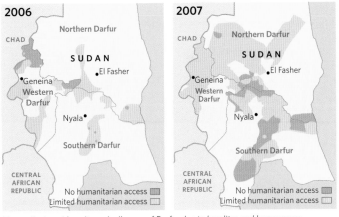

2006

CHAD
Northern Darfur
S U D A N
• El Fasher
• Geneina
Western Darfur
Nyala •
Southern Darfur
CENTRAL AFRICAN REPUBLIC

No humanitarian access
Limited humanitarian access

2007

CHAD
Northern Darfur
S U D A N
• El Fasher
• Geneina
Western Darfur
Nyala •
Southern Darfur
CENTRAL AFRICAN REPUBLIC

No humanitarian access
Limited humanitarian access

Humanitarian aid can't reach all areas of Darfur due to banditry and bureaucracy.

March 2003
Fighting breaks out between rebel groups and Sudanese government forces in Darfur, igniting the conflict.

April 8, 2004
The Sudanese government and the rebels sign a cease-fire agreement, including the deployment of African Union peacekeepers.

January 9, 2005
The separate, 21-year civil war officially ends with a comprehensive peace agreement between the government and the rebel group in southern Sudan.

May 5, 2006
A peace accord, which fails to end the conflict, is signed between the Sudanese government and a faction of the Sudan Liberation Army.

May 29, 2007
President Bush announces that the United States will impose economic sanctions on Sudan over the violence in Darfur.

2003   2004   2005   2006   2007

December 2003
A wave of attacks by the Janjaweed militia sends thousands of refugees into neighboring Chad.

May 24, 2004
The cease-fire agreement is broken as the government and the rebel factions blame each other for another village attack.

December 2005
The Darfur conflict spills over into neighboring Chad; the Chadian government accuses Sudan of supporting the violence there.

August 31, 2006
The UN Security Council passes a resolution to deploy a peacekeeping force in Darfur. Sudan rejects it, claiming it would violate national sovereignty.

July 31, 2007
The United Nations authorizes a 26,000-member hybrid peacekeeping force (UNAMID) for Darfur, which Sudan accepts.

Construction of the original oil pipeline in Persia, 1909

Enver Pasha

Mustafa Kemal Atatürk

1917
NOV. 2 Balfour Declaration asserts British government's support for the establishment of a national home for the Jewish people in Palestine.

1918
OCT. 3 Feisal sets up an Arab government in Damascus.

OCT. 30 Ottoman Empire signs armistice at Mudros.

NOV. Imamate of Yemen gains independence.

NOV. 11 Germany signs armistice.

1923
JULY 24 Treaty of Lausanne establishes modern Turkey's borders.

OCT. 29 Republic of Turkey is established. Mustafa Kemal Atatürk is named president; the capital is moved from Constantinople to Ankara.

1930
The collapse of the world pearl market following the Japanese introduction of cultured pearls leaves Qatar's economy in ruins.

1901
MAY 28 Shah Muzaffar al-Din of Persia grants a concession to British investor William Knox D'Arcy to drill for oil.

1906
AUG. 5 Constitutional Revolution lasting from 1905–1911 in Persia forces the shah to allow a constitution and a *Majlis*, or representative assembly.

1914
AUG. World War I (1914–1918) begins.

OCT. 29 Ottoman Empire enters war on the side of Germany by an alliance engineered by Enver Pasha, Ottoman War Minister.

DEC. 16 Egypt, under British military occupation since 1882, becomes a British protectorate. Cyprus is annexed by Great Britain.

1919
JAN. 18 Opening of Paris Peace Conference. The Treaty of Versailles is signed on June 28.

1925
MAY 1 Cyprus becomes a British Crown Colony.

DEC. 12 Pahlavi Dynasty in Persia is established when Reza Khan is crowned Reza Shah Pahlavi.

1933
MAY 29 King Abe ibn Saud allows S Oil to prospect in Saudi Arabia.

1902
Abdulaziz ibn Saud captures the city of Riyadh from the rival House of Rashid.

1907
AUG. 31 Great Britain and Russia sign an agreement that creates their respective spheres of influence in Persia.

1912-13
Balkan Wars result in the loss of most of the Ottoman Empire's remaining European territories.

1922
FEB. 28 Great Britain declares Egypt an independent monarchy. The Kingdom of Najd (Saudi Arabia) reaches boundary agreements with both Iraq and Kuwait.

1927
Large oil deposits are discovered north of Kirkuk in Iraq.

1934
DEC. 23 Oil explo concession in Ku is granted to Briti American-owned Kuwait Oil Comp

1903-05
An Anglo-Turkish Commission partially demarcates the boundary between Yemen (then part of the Ottoman Empire) and the British protectorate of Aden.

1909
Tel Aviv founded by Zionist settlers as a suburb of the ancient city of Jaffa.

1900

1910

1920

1930

1900
Germany and the Ottoman Empire begin construction of Pan-Islamic Hejaz Railway.

1908
MAY 26 First major oil strike occurs in the Middle East in southwest Persia at D'Arcy's drilling site at Masjid-i Suleman.

JULY 24 The Young Turk Revolution in the Ottoman Empire forces Sultan Abdul Hamid II to restore the Constitution of 1876.

Hejaz Railway is completed between Damascus and Medina.

1913
JUNE 21 First Arab National Congress, held in Paris, demands recognition of the Arabs as a nation within the Ottoman Empire.

Boundary between Iraq and Kuwait defined by Anglo-Turkish Convention.

1920
JAN. 16 League of Nations holds first meeting.

APR. 26 At San Remo Conference, Allied Powers endorse British mandates in Palestine and Iraq, and French mandate in Syria, a portion from which the French created Lebanon.

JULY 24 French oust Feisal from Damascus.

AUG. 10 Treaty of Sèvres reduces the Ottoman Empire to a small area of northern Anatolia.

1926
Boundary between Turkey and Iraq is settled by League of Nations initiative.

1932
SEPT. 18 Kingdom of Sa Arabia is proclaimed.

OCT. 3 Iraq is recognize as an independent mon following end of British mandate.

1904
APR. 8 Entente Cordiale: Agreement between Great Britain and France includes acknowledgment of British preeminence in Egypt.

JULY 3 Theodor Herzl dies; he founded the Zionist Organization at the First Zionist Congress in Basel, Switzerland, in 1897.

1915
APR. 24 Ottoman Empire launches genocide against the Armenians.

APR. 25 British Gallipoli Campaign begins, ending disastrously by Jan. 8, 1916.

1924
Abdulaziz ibn Saud captures Mecca, ousting Sharif Hussein. His conquest of the Hejaz is complete by 1926.

Abdulaziz ibn Saud, 1945

T.E. Lawrence

1916
MAY 16 Sykes-Picot Agreement: Secret treaty is made by France, Great Britain, and Russia to partition the Ottoman Empire.

JUNE Grand Sharif Hussein of Mecca launches Arab Revolt against Ottomans in the Hejaz. Military campaign is led by his son Feisal (later first king of Iraq) with British Army advisor T.E. Lawrence, known as Lawrence of Arabia.

NOV. Ruler of Qatar signs treaty of protection with Great Britain.

1921
FEB. 21 Reza Khan, an officer in the Persian Cossack Brigade, leads a successful coup in Persia.

APR. 1 Great Britain splits Palestine mandate to create Emirate of Transjordan and names Abdullah, son of Sharif Hussein, its ruler.

AUG. 23 Hashemite monarchy is established in Iraq under King Feisal I, whose Arab government was forced out of Damascus in July 1920.

1949
Qatar begins to produce and export oil ten years after discovering it.

FEB. 24 Armistice agreement is signed between Israel and Egypt, followed by armistices with other Arab countries later in the year.

1943
NOV. 22 Lebanon declares independence from France.

ⁿ Pahlavi changes
ame to Iran.

⁷
Y 7 British Peel
ⁿmmission recommends
t Palestine be partitioned.
e Woodhead Commission,
following year, rejects
ⁿtition as impracticable.

1945
MAR. 22 Arab League forms. World War II ends: Germany surrenders May 7; Japan surrenders Aug. 14.

OCT. 24 United Nations is founded.

1950
APR. 24 The West Bank is annexed by Transjordan, and the country's name is changed to Jordan.

▼ *Gamal Abdel Nasser in Damascus, 1960*

▼ *Israeli tank in action during the Six Day War*

1960
AUG. 15 Cyprus becomes an independent republic.

SEPT. 10-14 OPEC (Organization of Petroleum Exporting Countries) is founded in Baghdad by Iran, Iraq, Kuwait, Saudi Arabia, and Venezuela.

1967
JUNE 5-10 Six Day War: Following buildup of Arab troops on its borders and the closure of the Strait of Tiran, Israel launches a preemptive attack on the surrounding Arab states. Israel occupies the West Bank, including East Jerusalem, the Golan Heights, the Gaza Strip, and the Sinai Peninsula.

NOV. 30 Independent People's Democratic Republic of South Yemen forms.

⁹
T. 1 World War II
⁹39-1945) begins when Nazi
ⁿmany invades Poland.

1952
FEB. 18 Turkey is admitted as a member of NATO.

JULY 23 Gamal Abdel Nasser leads a coup by the Free Officers' Movement in Egypt. King Farouk is forced to abdicate.

1958
FEB. 22 Syria and Egypt form the United Arab Republic (U.A.R.).

JULY 14 King Feisal II of Iraq is assassinated in a coup by the army. General Qasim takes power.

JULY 15 U.S. Marines land in Lebanon to quiet Muslim-Christian civil strife.

1962
SEPT. 28 North Yemen becomes the Yemen Arab Republic. Civil war begins.

1964
JUNE 1 Palestinian Liberation Organization (PLO) is established.

AUG. 9 A cease-fire ends eight months of warfare between Greek and Turkish factions on Cyprus.

NOV. 2 King Saud is deposed. Faisal, his brother, succeeds him as King of Saudi Arabia.

1969
FEB. 3 Yasser Arafat is elected head of the PLO.

MAR. 17 Golda Meir becomes Prime Minister of Israel.

SEPT. 1 Monarchy in Libya is overthrown by military coup led by Muammar Qaddafi.

1941
MAY British troops invade Iraq to prevent coup by pro-Axis nationalist movement.

JUNE Invasion of Syria and Lebanon by British and Free French troops to remove the pro-Vichy France governments.

AUG. 25 British and Soviet troops occupy Iran to counter threat of expanding German influence. Reza Shah Pahlavi abdicates in favor of his son, Mohammad Reza Pahlavi.

1947
UN Partition Plan proposes that, upon termination of the British mandate on May 15, 1948, Palestine be partitioned into separate Jewish and Arab states, with the city of Jerusalem under UN control. Jews accept the plan. Arabs throughout the Middle East reject it.

Truman Doctrine results in large-scale U.S. military and economic aid to Turkey.

1955
FEB. 24 Baghdad Pact: Iraq allies itself with Turkey and Britain to contain Soviet expansionism.

1940   **1950**   **1960**   **1970**

36
ⁿG. 26 Anglo-Egyptian Treaty of
liance is signed. Formal British
ⁿcupation ends, though British
ⁿops remain in the Sinai and
ⁿz Canal Zone for 20 years.

ⁿR. 28 Farouk becomes
ⁿg following death of his
ⁿher King Fuad.

1942
OCT. 23-NOV. 4 British check German advance into Egypt at the Battle of El Alamein.

1953
JUNE Egypt is declared a republic.

AUG. 16-19 Prime Minister Mossadegh of Iran is overthrown by British-U.S. sponsored coup.

1961
JUNE 19 Kuwait, under Al Sabah family and British protectorate since 1899, gains independence. British troops sent in July to thwart an Iraqi attempt to annex Kuwait are later replaced by Arab League troops who remain there for two years.

SEPT. 28 Syria withdraws from the United Arab Republic. Egypt retains name until 1971.

1968
JULY 30 Baath Party returns to power in Iraq when a military coup led by President Ahmad Hasan al-Bakr ousts non-Baathist allies.

1938
Oil is discovered in Kuwait and Saudi Arabia.

NOV. 10 Mustafa Kemal Atatürk dies.

1946
APR. 17 Syria achieves complete independence.

MAY 15 Britain formally recognizes Transjordan as an independent state. Emir Abdullah becomes king.

1951
APR. 30 Mohammad Mossadegh becomes Prime Minister of Iran. He nationalizes British-owned oil industry.

JULY 20 King Abdullah of Jordan is assassinated.

1956
OCT. 31-NOV. 7 Suez Crisis: In a secret pact with Britain and France, Israel invades Sinai, reaching the Suez Canal. France and Britain land troops to "retake" canal. Pressure from U.S. and Soviet Union force withdrawal of invading forces.

1970
SEPT. King Hussein of Jordan sends army against PLO-controlled areas in Jordan. Defeated PLO retreats to Lebanon.

SEPT. 28 Egyptian President Nasser dies of a heart attack. He is succeeded by Vice President Anwar Sadat.

NOV. 13 Hafez al Assad seizes power in Syria as leader of a Baath Party military coup. Baath Party in Syria is a rival faction of Iraqi Baath Party.

NOV. 30 South Yemen is renamed People's Democratic Republic of Yemen.

DEC. Eight-year civil war in the Yemen Arab Republic (North Yemen) ends.

1948
MAY 14 State of Israel is proclaimed following end of British mandate in Palestine.

MAY 15 Israel's War of Independence: Arab forces from Egypt, Syria, Transjordan, Lebanon, and Iraq attack Israel, which defeats the invading armies. Many are uprooted by war, including 750,000 Palestinian refugees.

1963
JAN. 18 Former British colony of Aden joins Federation of South Arabia.

FEB. 8 In Iraq, General Qasim is overthrown in a Baath Party coup. Nine months later pro-Nasser military officers retake power from the Baath Party.

ⁿavid Ben-Gurion proclaims the birth of the State of
ⁿrael to the National Jewish Congress on May 14, 1948.

British recover hidden weapons in Suez Canal, 1956.

1971

AUG. 15 Bahrain declares independence.

SEPT. 3 Qatar declares its independence from Great Britain.

DEC. 2 Six of the Trucial States form the United Arab Emirates. The seventh joins the following year.

Israeli artillery engaged during Yom Kippur War

Khomeini's supporters on the streets of Tehran

1986

MAR. 24 U. S. Navy exercises in the Gulf of Sidra draw attacks from Libyan jets and patrol boats.

APR. 14 U. S. bombers attack military installation near Tripoli, Libya.

1984

FEB. 26 U. S. Marines withdraw from Lebanon.

MAY 20 Arab League condemns Iranian attacks on Persian Gulf shipping.

JUNE 5 Saudi jets down two Iranian planes over Persian Gulf.

AUG. 6 U.S. and British ships are sent to Gulf to clear mines. Russian, French, and Italian ships arrive within two weeks to keep shipping lanes open.

1973

OCT. 6 Yom Kippur War: Egypt and Syria launch surprise attack against Israel. After initial Arab victories Israel recaptures the Golan Heights, pushes six miles into Syria, and crosses the Suez Canal. Diplomatic interventions by the United States and Soviet Union lead to a cease-fire.

OCT. 20 Organization of Arab Petroleum Exporting Countries (OAPEC) imposes an oil embargo on the United States.

1977

MAY 17 Menachem Begin becomes Prime Minister of Israel.

NOV. 19-21 Egyptian President Anwar Sadat becomes the first Arab leader to visit Israel.

1979

JAN. 16 Mohammed Reza Shah Pahlavi leaves Iran due to mounting protests.

FEB. 1 Religious leader Ayatollah Ruhollah Khomeini returns from 15-year exile to establish an Islamic Republic in Iran.

MAR. 26 Egypt and Israel sign peace accords.

JULY 16 Saddam Hussein assumes Iraqi presidency.

NOV. 4 Militant Iranian students overrun U.S. Embassy in Tehran, taking 52 hostages.

DEC. 27 Soviet Union invades Afghanistan.

1981

JAN. 20 Iran releases all the American hostages.

JUNE 7 Israel bombs non-operational Iraqi nuclear reactor on the outskirts of Baghdad.

OCT. 6 Sadat is assassinated by Islamic fundamentalists in Egypt. Hosni Mubarak succeeds him as president.

DEC. 14 Israel annexes the Golan Heights.

1985

MAY-JUNE Israel withdraws from most of southern Lebanon to narrow security zone along the Israeli-Lebanese border.

OCT. 1 Israeli jets attack PLO headquarters in Tunis, Tunisia.

1975

MAR. 25 Saudi King Faisal is assassinated; his half brother, Crown Prince Khalid, succeeds him.

APR. Political and religious conflict between Christian and Muslim factions in Lebanon escalates into civil war.

1980

1972

NOV. 21 Israel and Syria clash in heaviest fighting since 1967 war.

JULY 18 Sadat expels Egypt's 15,000 Soviet military advisers and experts.

1974

MAR. 4 Israel returns Suez Canal to Egypt.

MAR. 18 OAPEC ends oil embargo.

JULY 15 Greece engineers coup in Cyprus.

JULY 20 Turkey invades Cyprus, occupying the northern one-third of the island.

NOV. 13 UN General Assembly affirms Palestinians' right to sovereignty and grants PLO observer status.

1976

APR.-MAY Syrian troops intervene in Lebanon to restore peace but also to curb the Palestinians.

OCT. Following Arab summit meetings in Riyadh and Cairo, a cease-fire in Lebanon is arranged and a predominantly Syrian Arab Deterrent Force (ADF) is established to maintain it.

1980

APR. 24 U.S. commandos' attempt to rescue hostages in Iran ends in failure.

JUNE Israel completes withdrawal to security zone in southern Lebanon.

SEPT. 22 Iraq invades Iran, beginning a war that lasts eight years.

1982

APR. 25 Israel completes withdrawal from Sinai.

JUNE 6 Israel invades Lebanon on "Operation Peace for Galilee."

AUG. 21-SEPT. 4 PLO evacuates Beirut during Israeli siege of the city.

SEPT. 18 Phalangist militia kill Palestinians in the Sabra and Shatila refugee camps.

SEPT. 24 The first contingent of a mainly U.S., French, and Italian peacekeeping force, requested by Lebanon, arrives in Beirut.

1987

The Islamic Resistance Movement, Hamas, is for from the Palestinian bran the Muslim Brotherhood.

DEC. 9 The first Palestinia uprising, or intifada, brea after an Israeli military tr kills four Palestinians in G

Sadat, Carter, and Begin at the White House, September 17, 1978

1978

MAR. 14 In reprisal for PLO attacks on its territory, Israel invades southern Lebanon.

APR. 6 United Nations Interim Force in Lebanon (UNIFIL) moves into southern Lebanon to enforce Security Council resolution calling on Israel to withdraw from Lebanon.

SEPT. 17 Camp David Accords are signed in Washington by Egyptian President Anwar Sadat and Israeli Prime Minister Menachem Begin with U.S. President Jimmy Carter as intermediary.

Iraqi soldiers at the front during the Iran-Iraq War

1983

APR. 18 Bomb blast destroys U.S. Embassy in Beirut, killing 63 people.

OCT. 23 Bomb blast destroys U.S. Marine barracks in Beirut, killing more than 300 soldiers and civilians.

NOV. 15 Turkish Republic of Northern Cyprus is declared. UN Security Council condemns the move.

American soldier stands on destroyed Iraqi tank while Kuwaiti oil wells burn in the distance.

Palestinians flee after throwing stones at Israeli army jeep during clashes in the West Bank.

Iraqi planes drop
[mustar]d gas and cyanide bombs
[on the] town of Halabja in ter-
[ritory] occupied by Iran. Nearly
[5,000] Iraqi Kurds are killed.

[Iran] accepts
[a dr]afted cease-fire plan to
[end ei]ght-year war with Iraq.

[King] King Hussein
[relinqu]ishes Jordan's claim
[to the] West Bank.

[Iraqi] Kurds flee to Turkey
[as reb]ellion is crushed in
[northe]rn Iraq.

[The] Palestinian National
[Counci]l (P.N.C.) proclaims an
[indepe]ndent Palestinian state.

[All] 270 people are killed
[when] Pan Am Flight 103 is
[bomb]ed; Libya is later accused
[of comp]licity.

1989
FEB. 15 Last Soviet troops leave Afghanistan.

JUNE 3 Ayatollah Ruhollah Khomeini of Iran dies.

1991
JAN. 17 Operation Desert Storm begins with a massive allied air attack against strategic targets in Baghdad and throughout Iraq.

FEB. 24 Allied coalition forces launch ground offensive into Iraq and occupied Kuwait.

FEB. 27 Kuwait is liberated. A cease-fire takes effect the next day. Retreating Iraqi troops set hundreds of oil wells on fire, causing an environmental disaster.

APR. 3 UN Security Council resolution requires Iraq to give up all chemical and biological weapons and materials for developing nuclear weapons. Iraq is required to provide arms inspection body UNSCOM complete access to all sites to monitor Iraqi disarmament.

1992
AUG. 27 Allied forces begin enforcing "no-fly zone" in southern Iraq, preventing Iraqi air attacks against the Shiite population.

1995
SEPT. 21 PLO and Israel sign Oslo II agreement.

NOV. 16 Israeli Prime Minister Yitzhak Rabin is assassinated by a Jewish religious extremist. His successor, Shimon Peres, vows to continue peace efforts.

1996
JAN. 20 Yasser Arafat is elected President of the Palestinian Authority.

JUNE 25 Islamic terrorists bomb Khobar Towers in Saudi Arabia, killing 19 Americans and one Saudi.

NOV. 29 Benjamin Netanyahu is elected Prime Minister of Israel.

1998
OCT. 23 Wye River Memorandum: Israel agrees to further troop withdrawals; the PLO to eliminate clauses from the PLO Covenant calling for Israel's destruction.

DEC. 17-20 U.S. and British warplanes bomb Iraq to force compliance with UNSCOM agreements. Following the attack Iraq refuses to readmit the UN weapons inspectors.

2000
MAY Israel completes withdrawal from security zone in southern Lebanon.

JUNE President Assad of Syria dies. He is succeeded by his son Bashar.

JULY 11-25 At Camp David II summit, Palestinian Authority leader Arafat and Israeli Prime Minister Barak fail to reach final peace settlement.

SEPT. 28 Second Palestinian uprising, the al Aqsa Intifada, begins in the Occupied Territories.

OCT. 12 USS Cole is bombed in Yemen by Islamic fundamentalists controlled by Osama bin Laden.

2002
JAN. 29 U.S. President George W. Bush declares Iran, Iraq, and North Korea "constitute an axis of evil."

MAR. Trying to stop a wave of suicide bombings, Israel reoccupies land it previously relinquished in the Occupied Palestinian Territories.

NOV. 8 UN Security Council Resolution 1441 calls on Iraq to disarm.

NOV. 21 UN weapons inspection team UNMOVIC resumes inspections in Iraq.

1990

2000

1990
MAY 22 The Republic of Yemen is created.

AUG. 2 Iraq invades Kuwait. UN Security Council condemns attack.

AUG. 7 Start of Operation Desert Shield; U.S.-led multinational coalition sends troops and supplies to Saudi Arabia to deter Iraqi attack.

NOV. 29 UN Security Council authorizes use of force against Iraq unless it withdraws from Kuwait by Jan. 15, 1991.

1993
AUG. During secret talks in Oslo, Norway, between Israel and the PLO, the Declaration of Principles (Oslo Accords) is announced. This agreement provides for Palestinian self-rule to be phased in over several years in the West Bank and the Gaza Strip.

SEPT. 13 Historic handshake between Israeli Prime Minister Rabin and PLO Chairman Arafat occurs at Oslo Accords signing ceremony hosted by U.S. President Bill Clinton on the White House lawn.

1994
MAY 4 PLO assumes authority in the Gaza Strip and town of Jericho. Israeli withdrawal begins two weeks later.

OCT. 13 Iraq deploys two divisions near border with Kuwait. Rapid deployment of U.S. forces in the area causes Iraq to withdraw troops.

OCT. 26 Jordanian King Hussein and Israeli Prime Minister Rabin sign formal peace treaty.

1997
JAN. 16 Israeli troops withdraw from West Bank town of Hebron the day after Israel signs Hebron Protocol with the Palestinian Authority.

1999
FEB. 7 King Hussein of Jordan dies. He is succeeded by his son Abdullah II.

JULY 6 Ehud Barak of the Labor Party replaces Netanyahu as Israeli Prime Minister.

JULY 23 King Hassan II of Morocco dies and is succeeded by his son Mohammed.

2001
FEB. 6 Ariel Sharon becomes Israeli Prime Minister.

SEPT. 11 Islamic terrorists hijack U.S. commercial jets and crash them into the World Trade Center in New York, and the Pentagon near Washington, D.C.

OCT. 7 U.S.-led military action starts in Afghanistan to remove the Taliban regime from power.

2003
JAN. 27 UNMOVIC and the IAEA report to the UN Security Council.

Saddam Hussein

Yasser Arafat returns to Gaza Strip on July 1, 1994.

Terrorists attack the World Trade Center on September 11, 2001.

▼ United States invades Iraq.

March 2003

1ST Khalid Sheikh Mohammed, key planner of 9/11 and other attacks, is captured.

11TH Turkish and Greek Cypriots fail to reunify before EU deadline after Tassos Papadopoulos is elected president.

20TH U.S., U.K., Australia, Denmark, and Poland attack Iraq with the support of 26 other countries.

April 2003

30TH "Road map for peace in the Middle East" is presented.

May 2003

1ST Magnitude 6.4 earthquake strikes Bingöl, Turkey, killing 167.

1ST Major combat in Iraq declared over by President Bush.

12TH Attacks on "western compounds" in Riyadh kill 35.

16TH Bombings by Moroccan Islamic extremists kill 45 in Casablanca.

October 2003

4TH Oman holds elections open to all adult citizens.

5TH Israel bombs guerrilla targets outside Damascus.

10TH Iranian woman Shirin Ebadi is awarded the Nobel Peace Prize for her work with democracy and women's and children's rights.

December 2003

12TH United States imposes economic sanctions on Syria.

13TH Saddam Hussein is captured in a spider hole near Tikrit, Iraq.

20TH Libya agrees to abandon its weapons of mass destruction programs.

26TH A magnitude 6.6 earthquake levels the city of Bam, Iran, killing 26,271.

January 2004

6TH Israel and Turkey agree to "Water for Arms" deal, sending fresh water from Turkey to Israel in exchange for Israeli tanks and aircraft.

Ghazi al-Yawar ▼

May 2004

1ST Greek Cyprus joins the European Union.

26TH A peace deal is signed between the Sudanese government and the S.P.L.A., ending a 20-year-old civil war — but it ignores Darfur.

June 2004

28TH Sovereignty is handed over to new Iraqi leadership of President Ghazi al-Yawar and Prime Minister Ayad Allawi.

28TH Iraq and Kuwait reestablish full diplomatic ties.

July 2004

9TH The International Court of Justice declares Israel's 437-mile barrier illegal.

14TH Ahmad Nazif becomes Prime Minister of Egypt, heading a cabinet tasked with economic reform.

▼ Danish cartoon protest

February 2005

Widespread demonstrations protest Danish cartoons depicting the prophet Muhammad.

10TH Saudi Arabia holds its first-ever elections, for municipal councils; only men are permitted to vote.

14TH Lebanon's former Prime Minister Rafik Hariri is assassinated in a car bombing, provoking mass demonstrations and widespread accusations of Syrian complicity.

28TH A Jordanian suicide bomber kills 120 in Al Hillah, triggering demonstrations in Iraq.

April 2005

6TH Iraqi Parliament elects Jalal Talabani as president, and Ibrahim al-Jaafari as prime minister.

17TH Northern Cyprus elects Mehmet Ali Talat as president.

26TH Syria completes the withdrawal from Lebanon of its military forces following pressure from the international community.

May 2005

16TH Women granted the r[...] vote in Kuwai[...]

2004   **2005**

June 2003

4TH Mahmoud Abbas, Ariel Sharon, and President Bush meet at a summit in Aqaba, Jordan, committed to peace. However, neither side upholds their end of the bargain.

21ST World Economic Forum meeting held in Aqaba.

July 2003

13TH A 25-member Iraqi Interim Governing Council is established.

22ND Saddam Hussein's sons Uday and Qusay are killed in a firefight in Mosul.

August 2003

15TH Libya accepts responsibility for the bombing of Pan Am Flight 103 in 1988 and agrees to compensate victims' families.

19TH A bomb explodes at UN headquarters in Baghdad, killing the top UN envoy to Iraq.

February 2004

1ST Abd al-Qadr Khan, leader of the Pakistani nuclear weapons program, admits to having run a campaign to sell nuclear technology to Iran, Libya, and North Korea.

18TH A runaway freight train in Neyshabur, Iran, derails and explodes, killing 195.

20TH Iran bans reformist candidates from running in elections.

March 2004

8TH Transitional Administrative Law proclaims Islam as a source of legislation and grants individual rights to all Iraqis.

11TH Terrorists linked to al Qaeda bomb commuter trains in Madrid, killing 191; a Moroccan is later convicted of involvement.

12TH Tension between Kurds and Baathists at a soccer match in northeastern Syria results in police shooting 12 Kurds, sparking riots in Kurdish areas of Syria.

20TH U.S. Army charges several members with assault and mistreatment of Iraqi prisoners at Abu Ghraib prison.

22ND Israel assassinates Hamas spiritual leader Ahmed Yassin as he leaves a mosque in Gaza.

April 2004

14TH "Disengagement Plan" is announced in Washington, D.C., in an attempt to negotiate an Israeli-Palestinian settlement.

January 2005

30TH The first general elections since occupation are h[...] in Iraq, producing a transitional National Assembly. Th[...] elections are largely boycotted by Sunni Arabs.

November 2004

2ND U.A.E.'s Sheikh Zayed ibn Sultan Al Nahyan dies, and is replaced by his eldest son Sheikh Khalifah ibn Zayed.

7TH Operation Phantom Fury begins, with an objective to recapture Fallujah from rebels and root out insurgents.

11TH Palestinian National Authority President Yasser Arafat dies.

July 2005

7TH Al Qaeda terrorist atta[...] the London underground an[...] kill 52 and injure 700.

19TH Fouad Siniora replaces [...] Mikati as Lebanese prime m[...]

20TH Bahrain ratifies a free [...] agreement with the United S[...]

23RD Three bombs in Sharm el Sheikh, Egypt, tourist areas kill 88.

Prisoner abuse at Abu Ghraib prison

Palestinians carrying posters and flags gather on Yasser Arafat's funeral day.

December 2005

8TH Ahmadinejad disputes that the Holocaust ever happened.

9TH Egpyt completes three rounds of parliamentary elections; the opposition Muslim Brotherhood wins 20 percent of seats.

11TH Saudi Arabia joins the World Trade Organization.

15TH General elections are held in Iraq, with the United Iraqi Alliance capturing the most seats and forming a coalition government.

005

King Fahd dies, and ed by Crown Prince

moud Ahmadinejad President of Iran.

el removes all set- za and from four ts in the West Bank.

ast 950 Shiite re killed in a stam- bridge in Baghdad, by shouts of a mber.

tember 2005

Egyptians elect ear president Hosni arak in the country's competitive idential election.

The last Israeli er leaves Gaza after -year occupation.

January 2006

4TH Israeli Prime Minister Ariel Sharon suffers brain hemorrhage and is replaced by Ehud Olmert.

4TH U.A.E. P.M. Sheikh Maktum ibn Rashid al-Maktum dies and is replaced by Sheikh Muhammad ibn Rashid al-Maktum.

9TH Mahmoud Abbas is elected to succeed Yasser Arafat as PLO President.

15TH Power struggle ensues in Kuwait after the death of Emir Sheikh Jabir al-Ahmad al-Jabir al-Sabah.

25TH Hamas wins a plurality in Palestinian legislative elections; President Abbas asks it to form a government.

February 2006

22ND Sunni-Shiite violence escalates after the bombing of a Shiite shrine in Samarra, pushing Iraq toward civil war.

Mahmoud Abbas

November 2006

23RD 215 killed in Sadr City bombings in Baghdad as Shiites commemorate Mohammad Mohammad Sadeq al-Sadr.

June 2006

25TH Palestinian militants in Gaza kidnap an Israeli soldier; Israel responds with a military attack.

December 2006

23RD UN Security Council imposes sanctions on Iran for its failure to comply with International Atomic Energy Agency demands that it stop enriching uranium.

30TH Saddam Hussein is executed.

Hamas rally

June 2007

13TH Iraqi Shiites bomb multiple Sunni mosques in response to the bombing of al-Askari pilgrimage shrine in Samarra.

15TH Hamas fighters take over Palestinian President Abbas's office and take Gaza by force, but pledge to work with Abbas.

September 2007

18TH Antoine Ghanem becomes the sixth anti-Syrian member of the Lebanese parliament to be assas- sinated since 2005.

October 2007

18TH In an assassination attempt, a suicide bomber attacks former Pakistani Prime Minister Benazir Bhutto's motorcade in Karachi, killing 139.

2006　　　　　　　　**2007**

er 2005

Oman and the United States sign a free trade ment.

A magnitude 7.6 earthquake strikes near Muzaf- ad, Pakistan, killing over 74,000.

A new Iraqi constitution is narrowly approved eferendum.

Ahmadinejad remarks in a speech that Israel t be wiped out from the map of the world."

mber 2005

Al Qaeda leader in Iraq, Abu Musab al-Zarqawi, ed by U.S. forces.

Several hotels in Amman are bombed by eda, killing 58.

Tempers flare over an incident in Haditha, Iraq, e 24 Iraqi civilians are killed by U.S. Marines in nse to a roadside bomb.

Marouf al-Bakhit becomes Prime Minister dan.

July 2006

11TH Commuter trains in Mumbai are attacked by terrorists from Pakistan.

12TH Hezbollah kidnaps two Israeli sol- diers; Israel responds with an attack on southern Lebanon. Over 1,000, mostly Lebanese civilians, are killed.

May 2006

20TH Nuri al-Maliki becomes Iraqi Prime Minister.

September 2006

20TH Yemen reelects 28-year president Major General 'Ali 'Abdallah Salih to another seven-year term.

April 2006
11TH Ahmadinejad announces that, despite protests from the European Union and the International Atomic Energy Agency, Iran has enriched uranium.

March 2007

13TH Ali Muhammad al-Mujawwar named Prime Minister of Yemen.

19TH The Egyptian parliament approves controversial amendments to the constitution infringing on human rights protections.

27TH Suicide truck bombing kills 152 in Tall Afar, Iraq.

April 2007

4TH Iran releases 15 British sailors after holding them for ten days when they crossed into Iranian waters.

18TH Iran produces enriched uranium, and vows that it is for peaceful purposes.

18TH Multiple bombings in Baghdad kill 198.

August 2007
28TH Turks elect as president Abdullah Gül of the Islamist- affiliated Justice and Development Party.

December 2007

3RD U.S. intelligence agencies report that Iran had halted its nuclear weapons development program in 2003.

18TH Multiple bombings in Baghdad kill 198.

27TH Benazir Bhutto is assassinated after a politi- cal rally, just weeks before a scheduled Pakistani national election.

Muzaffarabad earthquake

Mahmoud Ahmadinejad

Baghdad car bombings

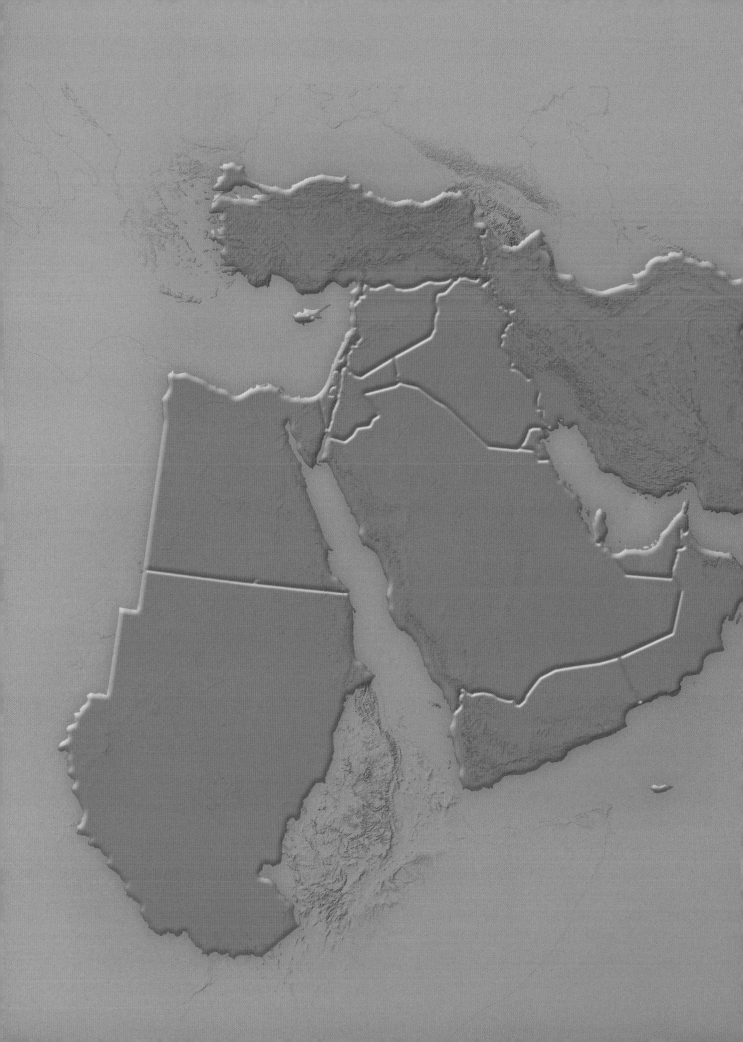

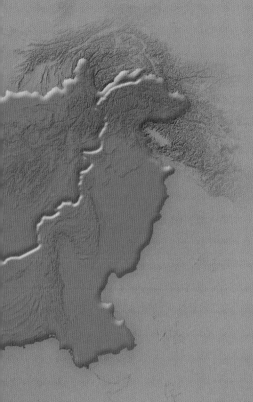

Appendix

LEFT TO RIGHT: The Iranian short-range missile Shahab-2 is displayed next to the poster of Supreme Leader Ayatollah Ali Khamenei during the 27th anniversary of the outset of the Iran-Iraq war; A GOSP2 (Gas Oil Separation Plant) burns off excess gas that cannot be sent to the refinery at the oil field in Shaybah, Saudi Arabia; From left to right: Egypt's President Hosni Mubarak, Iraq's President Jalal Talabani, and Qatar's Sheikh Hamad bin Khalifa al-Thani attend the opening ceremony of the 19th Arab League Summit in Riyadh, March 2007; Kurdish refugee children pose for a photo in front of a damaged mural of Saddam Hussein; Kuwait Towers, Kuwait City

Flags of the Middle East
Colors of Islam

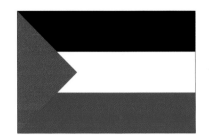

BY WHITNEY SMITH

FOUR COLORS HAVE BEEN associated for centuries with banners used by the Islamic dynasties — the Umayyads (white), Abbasids (black), Fatimids (green), and the Ottomans (red) — who successively ruled Islamic countries from the beginning of Islam in the seventh century. Each used an event in the life of the Prophet to justify their claims to be his proper successor. For example, Fatima, the daughter of Muhammad, was said always to have worn green clothing, and the Fatimid dynasty took this as a sign of its legitimacy.

The 14th-century poet Safi al-Din al-Hilli explained the meaning of those four colors:

White (pure) are our deeds, black (deadly) are our battles, green (fruitful) are our fields, and red (bloody) are our knives.

So strong were those traditions for Muslims, even today few countries in the Muslim world have flags that include other than those four hues. In the Middle Ages Christians and Jews living in Muslim territories were required to wear badges to show that they were not part of the dominant culture.

At the beginning of the 20th century Arab youths and intellectuals combined those colors to represent the Arab past and their desire for future Arab unity and freedom. When World War I started in 1914 the sharif of the Hejaz championed the pan-Arab independence movement under what was known as the Arab Revolt flag. Britain and its European allies denied

AFGHANISTAN UNDER TALIBAN Following the 1989 retreat of Soviet armed forces from Afghanistan, different political factions struggled for control over the country. The Taliban, committed to fundamentalist Islam, imposed its rule over 90% of the country before American and allied forces intervened. The Taliban still controls various parts of Afghanistan.

ARAB LEAGUE The color green and the crescent are symbols often used by member countries of the League of Arab States. Founded in 1945, the League works to coordinate policies and activities of its members for greater effectiveness.

GULF COOPERATION COUNCIL The Cooperation Council of the Arab States of the Gulf was organized in 1981 to promote regional development under the map and flag colors of the Middle East. The Arabian Peninsula is represented within the inscription: "In the name of Allah, the All-Merciful."

HEZBOLLAH Islamic fundamentalists were able to establish rule over parts of Lebanon and all of the Gaza Strip during 2007. Although unrecognized by any other government, Hezbollah continues to control the captured territories, providing a base for further military assaults on neighboring territories.

ISLAM Because Muslims believe that the word of Allah is expressed in the Holy Koran, its text is considered to be sacred. Here the words "There is no God but Allah; Muhammad is the Prophet of Allah" appear as the fundamental creed of Islam displayed on a widely used but unofficial flag.

KURDISTAN During the 1991 gulf war, Kurds in northern Iraq de facto established self-rule. The flag used unofficially for decades was adopted in modified form in 1999 by the Kurdish regional government in northern Iraq. Kurds are the largest ethnic minority in the world without their own independent country.

MULTINATIONAL FORCE AND OBSERVERS The MFO has successfully monitored the border between Egypt and Israel since 1982. The designer of the logo and flag intentionally chose orange as a neutral color. The stylized dove and olive branch traditionally symbolize peace.

ORGANIZATION OF THE ISLAMIC CONFERENCE The traditional green of the cloak of the Prophet Muhammad and his daughter, Fatima, has frequently been used in Muslim flags. The flag of the Islamic Conference adds a red crescent. The motto "God Is Almighty" and a stylized globe symbolize this worldwide Muslim organization.

ORGANIZATION OF THE PETROLEUM EXPORTING COUNTRIES (OPEC) Organized in 1960, the cartel works to coordinate the policies of countries where petroleum is a major export product. Its flag, adopted in 1970, consists of a blue background of the same shade as the United Nations flag with stylized versions of the initials O, P, E, and C.

PALESTINIANS A combination of the four most widely respected Muslim flag colors was chosen in 1922 by the Palestinians for their flag. The red, white, green, and black are the traditional Arab dynastic colors, a symbol of the statehood Palestinians have long desired.

ARAB REVOLT FLAG On May 30, 1916, the sharif of the Hejaz and protector of the holy sites of Islam, Mecca and Medina, proclaimed Arab independence from Turkish rule. A year later the Arab Revolt flag (left) was first officially hoisted as a national banner for all Arab lands. Its stripes of black, green, and white represented historical Arab dynasties, linked by the sharif's triangular red flag. In 1922, the positions of the green and white stripes were reversed to make the flag more visible at a distance.

Arabs their indepedence. Nevertheless the flag of black, white, and green stripes with a red triangle at the hoist continued to inspire Arab nationalists.

After the Second World War the new Arab Liberation Flag appeared in different versions to inspire Muslims. The first one, horizontal stripes of red-white-black, was raised by Egyptians to symbolize their struggles against foreign imperialism and for domestic modernization and democracy. In 1958 Syrians and Egyptians jointly adopted the Arab Liberation Flag charged with two green stars. Other attempts at unity hoisted similar designs, including the 2008 Iraqi flag.

Even today most Muslim flags are based on the standards that were carried by Muhammad or by his associates. The colors of those Islamic flags were originally based on oral history, later preserved by scholars in manuscripts.

The four basic colors of the dynasties are directly based on those traditions. Thus the flag color of the governors of Mecca, red, helped legitimize the red of the Ottoman dynasty, which was Turkic, not Arab.

Today the black and white colors of al Qaeda, which is trying to reestablish the caliphate (the religious institution that in the Middle Ages was the sole authority for civil as well as religious issues), are reminicent of flag traditions dating back 700 years.

AL QAEDA A common version of the flag of al Qaeda, which means "the Base," resembles one in use by Muhammad in the seventh century — black wool with the Shahada (Testimony) inscribed on it. It reads: "There is no god except Allah [God]; Muhammad is the Prophet of Allah." The Shahada emphasizes the oneness of God and belief that Muhammad is his final prophet. The calligraphy of the original flag contrasts with the same text in *thuluth* script, as in the Islam flag.

RED CRESCENT In Muslim nations, Geneva Convention organizations rejected the red cross in favor of a red crescent, officially recognized in 1906. The Red Crescent and Red Cross are sometimes shown together in countries with both Muslims and non-Muslims.

RED CROSS The Geneva Convention developed out of the Red Cross Society, which was designed by Jean-Henri Dunant. Formalized through the Convention, this international organization recognized a red cross as its symbol for use on uniforms, vehicles, and buildings protected by international treaty during wartime.

RED CRYSTAL The official medical services organization of Israel since 1948 has been used in times of national catastrophe and war. It was not recognized by the Geneva Conventions, however. In 2006, an agreement was reached whereby the Red Crystal would be recognized with other Geneva Convention symbols.

SOUTHERN SUDAN For centuries Muslim Sudanese obtained slaves from upper Nile regions. A revolt by Christians and animists forced the Sudan government to grant broad local autonomy to Southern Sudan in 2006. A referendum may eventually determine if Southern Sudan is to become an independent country.

SOVEREIGN BASE AREAS Since 1960 the United Kingdom, by treaty, has exercised sovereignty over parts of the Republic of Cyprus in order to maintain peace. Those special areas display the Union Jack, national flag of Great Britain.

SUEZ AUTHORITY The modern Suez Canal, completed in 1869, was under European control. In 1956 Egypt nationalized the canal, provoking an attack by Britain, France, and Israel. Although the canal still carries heavy traffic under its flag, the geopolitical importance of the canal has been diminished in recent decades.

TURKISH REPUBLIC OF NORTHERN CYPRUS In 1970 Turkey occupied Turkish-populated areas of Cyprus, and in 1983 that area unilaterally proclaimed itself an independent state called the Turkish Republic of Northern Cyprus. Its flag is based on the one used by Turkey.

UNITED NATIONS Olive branches, for centuries a symbol of peace, were combined with a world map to form the symbol adopted by the United Nations the year after its creation. The UN flag today is found in peacekeeping missions, health programs, and conferences dedicated to solving international problems.

UNITED STATES CENTRAL COMMAND Increasing military engagements on the part of the United States led its Department of Defense to establish the U.S. Central Command in January 1983. The gulf war and the U.S. invasion of Afghanistan and Iraq resulted in expansion of that command. The American eagle symbolizes defense of American interests in the Middle East, as reflected in the stylized background map.

Place-Name Index

The following system is used to locate a place on a map in this atlas. The boldface type after an entry refers to the page on which the map is found; the letter-number combination refers to the grid on which the particular place-name is located. The edge of each map is marked horizontally with numbers and vertically with letters. In between, at equally spaced intervals, are small triangles. If these small triangles were connected with lines, each page would be divided into a grid. Take the town of Muratlı, for example. The index entry reads "Muratlı, *Turkey* **56 B2** ." On page 56, Muratlı is located within the grid square where row B and column 2 intersect (see diagram, right).

A place-name may appear on several maps, but the index lists only the best presentation. Usually, this means that a feature is indexed to the largest-scale map on which it appears in its entirety. (Note: Rivers are often labeled multiple times even on a single map. In such cases, the rivers are indexed to labels that are closest to their mouths.) The name

of the country or continent in which a feature lies is shown in italic type and is sometimes abbreviated.

Some entries include a feature description shown in purple, as in "Forūr, island, *Iran* **32 L7** ." When a feature or place can be referred to by more than one name, both may appear in the index with cross-references. For example, the entry for Constantinople reads "Constantinople *see* İstanbul, *Turk.* **56 B4**." That entry is "İstanbul (Constantinople), *Turk.* **56 B4**."

Abbreviations:

mts.	*mountains*
pen.	*peninsula*
plat.	*plateau*
sett.	*settlement*

Examples:

feature description ⟶
Lîtâni, river, *Leb.* **42 L2** ⟵ page number / grid coordinate / country

feature name ⟶
Haiya, *Sudan* **53 C10** ⟵ page number / grid coordinate

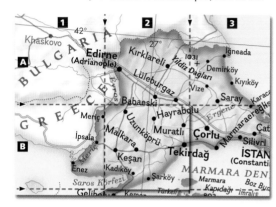

Aadaïssé, *Leb.* **42** L3
Aajaltoûn, *Leb.* **42** F4
Aaley, *Leb.* **42** G3
Aalma ech Chaab, *Leb.* **42** MI
Aanjar, *Leb.* **42** H5
Aarsal, *Leb.* **42** D8
Abā as Sa'ūd, *Saudi Arabia* **50** L6
Ababdah, Jebel, *Sudan* **53** CIO
Ābādān, *Iran* **32** H3
Ābādeh, *Iran* **32** H5
Abâr el Kanâyis, well, *Egypt* **30** C3
Abarkūh, *Iran* **32** H6
Abasān al Kabīr, *Gaza Strip* **62** LI
Abayd, Lake, *Sudan* **52** H6
Abbottabad, *Pak.* **47** C9
'Abd al 'Azīz, Jabal, *Syr.* **54** C9
'Abdalī, site, *Kuwait* **41** A7
'Abd al Kūrī, island, *Yemen* **61** HI5
Ab-e Istadeh-ye Moqor, lake, *Afghan.* **25** H7
Abhā, *Saudi Arabia* **50** L5
'Abidiya, *Sudan* **52** C9
Abū Ḥulayfah, *Kuwait* **41** HIO
Abnûb, *Egypt* **31** G7
Abou Aali, river, *Leb.* **42** C5
Abrād, Wādī, *Yemen* **60** E6
Abraq al Ḥabārī, escarpment, *Kuwait* **40** F3
Abraq Khaytān, *Kuwait* **41** G9
Abrūq, Ra's, *Qatar* **48** E4
Abū aḍ Ḍuhūr, *Syr.* **54** D3
Abū 'Ajram, *Saudi Arabia* **50** C3
Abū al Abyaḍ, island, *U.A.E.* **59** G6
Abū al 'Awsaj, region, *Bahrain* **27** F7
Abū al Ḥuṣayn, Qā', *Jordan* **39** EIO
Abū 'Alī, island, *Saudi Arabia* **50** E9
Abū al Khaṣīb, *Iraq* **35** KII
Abū al Lasan, *Jordan* **38** K3
Abū 'Arīsh, *Saudi Arabia* **50** L5
Abū 'Awdah, peak, *Gaza Strip* **62** MI
Abu 'Aweiḍ, Râs, *Egypt* **31** HIO
Abū aẓ Ẓulūf, *Qatar* **48** B5
Abū Bahām, *Bahrain* **27** B7
Abū Bahr, region, *Saudi Arabia* **50** H8
Abū Ballâs, peak, *Egypt* **30** J3
'Abūd, *W. Bank* **63** F6
Abū Daghmah, *Syr.* **54** C5
Abū Dālī, *Syr.* **54** G3
Abu Deleiq, *Sudan* **52** E8
Abu Dhabi, *U.A.E.* **59** F8
Abū Dīs, *W. Bank* **63** H8
Abu Dis, *Sudan* **52** C8

Abu Dukhân, Gebel, *Egypt* **31** G9
Abu Durba, *Egypt* **31** E9
Abu el Ḥusein, Bîr, *Egypt* **31** L6
Abu Gabra, *Sudan* **52** H5
Abu Gamal, *Sudan* **53** EIO
Abu Gharâdiq, Bîr, *Egypt* **31** D4
Abu Gubeiha, *Sudan* **52** G7
Abu Hamed, *Sudan* **52** B8
Abū Hāmūr, *Qatar* **48** G7
Abū Harba, Gebel, *Egypt* **31** G9
Abu Hashaifa, Khalîg, *Egypt* **31** C4
Abū Jarjūr, Ra's, *Bahrain* **27** D8
Abū Kamāl, *Syr.* **55** GIO
Abū Madd, Ra's, *Saudi Arabia* **50** F2
Abu Mareiwât, Bîr, *Egypt* **31** G9
Abu Matariq, *Sudan* **52** H5
Abu Minqâr, Bîr, *Egypt* **30** G3
Abu Musa, island, *Iran, U.A.E.* **59** B9
Ābūr, *Jordan* **38** H4
Abu Rudeis, *Egypt* **31** E8
Abu Saiyal, well, *Sudan* **52** D7
Abū Samrah, *Qatar* **48** K4
Abu Shagara, Ras, *Sudan* **53** AIO
Abū Shanab, *Sudan* **52** F5
Abū Sidrah, *Qatar* **48** D4
Abu Simbel, site, *Egypt* **31** L7
Abū Sôma, Râs, *Egypt* **31** G9
Abū Sufyan, *Sudan* **52** G5
Abū Şukhayr, *Iraq* **35** H7
Abu Tabari, well, *Sudan* **52** D6
Abu Tîg, *Egypt* **31** G7
Abu 'Uruq, *Sudan* **52** E7
Abu Zabad, *Sudan* **52** G6
Abu Zenîma, *Egypt* **31** E8
'Abwayn, *W. Bank* **63** E7
Abwong, *Sudan* **52** J8
Abyad, *Sudan* **52** F5
Abyad, El Bahr el (White Nile), *Sudan* **52** G8
Abyad Plateau, Jebel, *Sudan* **52** C6
Abyei, *Sudan* **52** H6
Abyek, *Iran* **32** D4
Achna, *N. Cyprus* **28** G6
Acıgöl, lake, *Turk.* **56** F4
Acıpayam, *Turk.* **56** F4
Acre *see* 'Akko, *Israel* **36** C4
Adalia *see* Antalya, *Turk.* **56** G5
Adam, *Oman* **45** F8
Adam Bridge, *W. Bank* **63** EIO
'Adan (Aden), *Yemen* **60** H6
Adana, *Turk.* **56** G9
'Adan aş Şughrá, cape, *Yemen* **60** H6

Adapazarı *see* Sakarya, *Turk.* **56** B5
Aḍ Ḍafrah, desert, *U.A.E.* **58** J3
Ad Daghghārah, *Iraq* **35** H8
Ad Dahnā', desert, *Saudi Arabia* **50** D6
Aḍ Ḍali', *Yemen* **60** G5
Ad Damer, *Sudan* **52** D9
Ad Dammām, *Saudi Arabia* **50** E9
Ad Dār al Ḥamrā, *Saudi Arabia* **50** D2
Ad Darb, *Saudi Arabia* **50** L5
Ad Dawādimī, *Saudi Arabia* **50** F6
Ad Dawḥah (Doha), *Qatar* **48** G7
Ad Dawḥah (Doha), *Kuwait* **41** F8
Ad Dawr, *Iraq* **35** E7
Ad Dayr, *Bahrain* **27** A8
Ad Dibdibah, region, *Kuwait* **40** F3
Ad Dibdibah, region, *Saudi Arabia* **50** D7
Aḍ Ḍiffah, plateau *see* Libyan Plateau, *Egypt* **30** CI
Ad Dilam, *Saudi Arabia* **50** G7
Ad Dirāz, *Bahrain* **27** B6
Ad Dīwānīyah, *Iraq* **35** H8
Aḍ Ḍubā'īyah, *Kuwait* **41** JIO
Ad Dujayl, *Iraq* **35** F7
Ad Dūr, *Bahrain* **27** F8
Ad Durra, *Jordan* **38** M2
Ad Duwayd, *Saudi Arabia* **50** C5
Adelfoi, peak, *Cyprus* **28** H3
Aden *see* 'Adan, *Yemen* **60** H6
Aden, Gulf of, *Ind. Oc.* **21** KIO
Adhanah, Wādī, *Yemen* **60** F5
Adh Dhakhīrah, *Qatar* **48** D7
Ādhirīyāt, Jibāl al, *Jordan* **38** H6
'Adiyah, Jabal, *Yemen* **60** E5
Adıyaman, *Turk.* **57** FI2
Adraskan, *Afghan.* **24** G2
Adrianople *see* Edirne, *Turk.* **56** A2
'Afak, *Iraq* **35** H8
Afghanistan, *Asia* **23** CI4
'Afif, *Saudi Arabia* **50** G5
Afiq, *Israel* **36** C6
Afqa, *Leb.* **42** E5
'Afrīn, *Syr.* **54** C3
Afşin, *Turk.* **57** FII
'Afula, *Israel* **36** D4
Afyon, *Turk.* **56** E5
Aghbar, Jabal al, *Yemen* **60** G4
Aghûrmi, *Egypt* **30** E2
Agia Napa, *Cyprus* **28** H6
Agios Amvrosios, *N. Cyprus* **28** F5

Agios Athanasios, *Cyprus* **28** J3
Agios Dometios, *Cyprus* **28** G4
Agios Sergios, *N. Cyprus* **28** G6
Agios Theodoros, *N. Cyprus* **28** F6
Aglangia, *Cyprus* **28** G4
Agri (Karaköse), *Turk.* **57** CI6
Ağrı Dağı (Mount Ararat), *Turk.* **57** CI7
Ahar, *Iran* **32** B2
Ahlat, *Turk.* **57** EI6
Ahlatlıbel, ruin, *Turk.* **56** D7
Ahmadpur East, *Pak.* **47** H8
Ahmad Wal, *Pak.* **47** G4
Aḥmar, Jabal al, *Jordan* **38** L2
Ahram, *Iran* **32** J5
Āhū, *Iran* **32** H3
Ahvāz, *Iran* **32** G3
Aḥwar, *Yemen* **60** G8
Aigialousa, *N. Cyprus* **28** E7
Aïnâta, *Leb.* **42** D6
Ajban, *U.A.E.* **59** F9
'Ajīrah, Jazīrat, *Bahrain* **27** JII
'Ajjah, *W. Bank* **63** C7
'Ajlūn, *Jordan* **38** C4
'Ajmān, *U.A.E.* **59** DIO
Ajrestan, *Afghan.* **25** G6
'Ajūzah, Ra's al, *Kuwait* **41** F9
Aka, river, *Sudan* **52** M6
Akanthou, *N. Cyprus* **28** F6
'Akāshāt, *Iraq* **34** F2
Akçaabat, *Turk.* **57** BI3
Akçadağ, *Turk.* **57** EI2
Akçakale, *Turk.* **57** GI3
Akçakışla, *Turk.* **57** DIO
Akçakoca, *Turk.* **56** B6
Akçay, *Turk.* **56** D2
Akçay, *Turk.* **56** G4
Akdağ, peak, *Turk.* **56** EI
Ak Dağları, peak, *Turk.* **56** H4
Akdağmadeni, *Turk.* **57** DIO
Akelo, *Sudan* **52** K8
Akhḍar, Al Jabal al, *Oman* **45** E8
Akhisar, *Turk.* **56** D3
Akhmîm, *Egypt* **31** G7
Akhtarîn, *Syr.* **54** C4
'Akko (Acre), *Israel* **36** C4
Akkuş, *Turk.* **57** BII
Akobo, *Sudan* **52** K8
Ākobo, river, *Sudan* **52** K9
Akot, *Sudan* **52** K7
Akrotiri, *Cyprus* **28** J3
Akrotiri Bay, *Cyprus* **28** J3

Akrotiri Sovereign Base Area, *Cyprus* **28** J3
Akrūm, ruin, *Leb.* **42** B7
Aksaray, *Turk.* **56** E8
Akşehir, *Turk.* **56** E6
Akşehir Gölü, *Turk.* **56** E6
Akseki, *Turk.* **56** G6
'Aksha, ruin, *Egypt* **31** M7
Aksu, river, *Turk.* **56** G5
Akyaka, *Turk.* **57** BI7
Akyazı, *Turk.* **56** B5
Al 'Abdalīyah, *Kuwait* **41** H7
Alaca, *Turk.* **56** C9
Alaca Dağ, *Turk.* **56** F6
Alacahöyük, ruin, *Turk.* **56** C9
Alaçam, *Turk.* **57** AIO
Aladağ, peak, *Turk.* **56** F6
Aladağ, peak, *Turk.* **56** F9
Al 'Adā'im, ruin, *Bahrain* **27** F6
Al Ad'amī, *Kuwait* **41** KII
Al 'Adhbah, *Qatar* **48** B6
Al Aflāj, mts., *Saudi Arabia* **50** H7
Al Aḥmadī, *Kuwait* **41** H9
Al Ain, *U.A.E.* **59** GII
Al Akhḍar, *Saudi Arabia* **50** D2
Al 'Akr, *Bahrain* **27** C8
Alalakh, ruin, *Turk.* **57** HIO
Al 'Amar, *Bahrain* **27** F7
Al 'Amārah, *Iraq* **35** HIO
Al Amarat, *Oman* **45** E8
'Alam el Rûm, Râs, *Egypt* **30** C3
Al 'Āmirīyah, *Qatar* **48** K5
'Alam Lek, *Afghan.* **25** C5
Alandar, *Afghan.* **25** F5
Alanya, *Turk.* **56** H6
Al 'Aqabah (Aqaba), *Jordan* **38** L2
Al 'Aqīq, *Saudi Arabia* **50** J4
Alara, river, *Turk.* **56** G6
Al 'Āriḍīyah, *Kuwait* **41** G8
Al 'Arīsh, *Qatar* **48** B5
Al 'Armah, region, *Saudi Arabia* **50** E7
Al Arṭawīyah, *Saudi Arabia* **50** E6
Al Āş (Orontes), river, *Syr.* **54** F2
Al As'ad, *Saudi Arabia* **50** D2
Alaşehir, *Turk.* **56** E3
Al 'Ashārah, *Syr.* **55** FIO
Al Ashkharah, *Oman* **45** F9
Al Atārib, *Syr.* **54** D3
Al Awaya, *Oman* **45** L3
'Alawīyīn, Jabal al, *Syr.* **54** E2

Acknowledgments

REGIONAL THEMES

Climate pp. 72-73
CONSULTANTS
David Lister, University of East Anglia
Murray Peel, The University of Melbourne
GRAPHICS
CLIMATE ZONES: Peel, M. C., Finlayson, B. L., and McMahon, T. A.: Updated world map of the Köppen-Geiger climate classification, *Hydrol. Earth Syst. Sci.*, 11, 1633-1644, 2007. **MEAN TEMPERATURE AND PRECIPITATION:** The CGIAR Consortium for Spatial Information (CGIAR-CSI). CRU TS 2.1 Climate Database (available at http://cru.csi.cgiar.org).

Land Cover pp. 74-75
CONSULTANT
Mark Friedl, Dept. of Geography and Environment, Boston University
GRAPHICS
LAND COVER DISTRIBUTION: Boston University Department of Geography and Environment Global Land Cover Project. Source data provided by NASA's Moderate Resolution Imaging Spectroradiometer. Pie chart data processing by Damien Sulla-Menashe.

Population pp. 76-77
CONSULTANTS
Carl Haub, Population Reference Bureau (PRB)
Greg Yetman, Center for International Earth Science Information Network (CIESIN) Columbia University
GENERAL REFERENCES
Center for International Earth Science Information Network (CIESIN), Columbia University: www.ciesin.org; U.S. Census Bureau; *World Urbanization Prospects and World Population Prospects.* Division of the Department of Economic and Social Affairs of the United Nations Secretariat: esa.un.org/unup
GRAPHICS
POPULATION DENSITY: Center for International Earth Science Information Network (CIESIN), Columbia University, and Centro Internacional de Agricultura Tropical (CIAT), 2005. Gridded Population of the World Version 3 (GPWv3): Population Density Grids—World Population Density, 2005 [map]. Palisades, New York: Socioeconomic Data and Applications Center (SEDAC), Columbia University. Accessed October 2007. Available at http://sedac.ciesin.columbia.edu/gpw

Urbanization pp. 78-79
GENERAL REFERENCES
Center for International Earth Science Information Network (CIESIN), Columbia University: www.ciesin.org; U.S. Census Bureau; *World Urbanization Prospects and World Population Prospects.* Division of the Department of Economic and Social Affairs of the United Nations Secretariat: esa.un.org/unup. Dubai: Sudden City, *National Geographic* magazine, January 2007.

Religion pp. 80-81
CONSULTANTS
Robert William Hefner, Boston University
M.R. Izady
Todd Johnson, Center for the Study of Global Christianity

GENERAL REFERENCES
World Christian Database, 2007 (available at http://worldchristiandatabase.org/wcd).
GRAPHICS
RELIGIONS OF THE MIDDLE EAST: Compilation by M.R. Izady, based on the following sources: Largely, Government of Turkey, Statistical Bureau, *Köy Envanter Etudleri* (1961-64); A. Razmara, *Farhang-i jughrafiyi-i Iran* (1949-51); P. Andrews, ed., *Ethnic Groups in Republic of Turkey* (1989), L. Dupree, Afghanistan (1973); Bruk, *Narody Peredney Azii* (1960); *Annual Abstract of Statistics, 1970* (Baghdad: Government of Iraq, 1971); *Weltkarte, Sonderausgabe: Volkstum* (Vienna, 1943-44); *Les Tribus Arabes de Syrie* (Damascus: Government of French Mandate of Syria, Section d'étude du service des renseignments du Levant, 1930). British Naval Intelligence Division, *Iraq and the Persian Gulf* (1944); J.G. Lorimer, *Gazetteer of the Persian Gulf, Oman and Central Arabia* (1986); *British administration reports for Mesopotamia, Iraq Administration Reports 1914-1932,* reprint 1992; B. Destani, ed., *Minorities in the Middle East: Christian Minorities 1838-1967* (2007); B. Destani, ed., *Minorities In The Middle East: Druze Communities 1840-1974* (2006); R. Trench, *Gazetteer Of Arabian Tribes* (1996); B. Destani, ed., *Minorities In The Middle East: Muslim Minorities In Arab Countries 1843-1973* (2007); A. Burdett, *Afghanistan Strategic Intelligence Records 1919-1970* (2006); M.R. Izady, *The Kurds: A Concise Handbook* (1992); Joshua Project (for the Christian communities of Sudan).

Language and Ethnic Groups pp. 82-83
CONSULTANT
M.R. Izady
GRAPHICS
LANGUAGES OF THE MIDDLE EAST: See source compilation by M.R. Izady for Religions of the Middle East (above).

Oil pp. 84-85
CONSULTANT
Ronald Jansen, United Nations Statistics Division
GENERAL REFERENCES
Energy Information Administration (EIA): http://www.eia.doe.gov; EIA , Office of Energy Markets End Use, 2006 estimates; PennWell Corportaion, Oil and Gas Journal; January 1, 2007.
GRAPHICS
ENERGY RESOURCES: PennWell International Petroleum Encyclopedia, 2007. **LEADING CRUDE OIL PRODUCERS GRAPH:** EIA, *International Petroleum Monthly,* July 2007. **MIDDLE EAST EXPORTS AND GLOBAL OIL CONSUMPTION:** COMTRADE: http://comtrade.un.org

Water pp. 86-87
CONSULTANTS
Christopher Gasson, Global Water Intelligence
Peter H. Gleick, Pacific Institute
W. Struckmeier, BGR International Cooperation, Groundwater
C.J. Vörösmarty and Pamela Green, University of New Hampshire
GENERAL REFERENCES
Pacific Institute, 2007; Millennium Development Goals (UN-MDG): www.un.org/millenniumgoals

GRAPHICS
GROUNDWATER RESOURCES: World-wide Hydrogeological Mapping and Assessment Programme (WHYMAP), BGR & UNESCO (available at http://www.whymap.org); Global Water Intelligence (available at http://www.globalwaterintel.com) **POPULATION DENSITY AND WATER STRESS:** P.A. Green, C.J. Vörösmarty, and colleagues, Water Systems Analysis Group, University of New Hampshire; www.wsag.unh.edu; 2000 data. **DESALINATION CAPACITY:** Global Water Intelligence: http://www.globalwaterintel.com; http://desaldata.com

Food and Agriculture pp. 88-89
CONSULTANT
Freddy Nachtergaele, Food and Agricultural Organization (FAO)
GENERAL REFERENCES
FAO Statistical Yearbook, 2005-2006: http://www.fao.org/ES/ess/yearbook; FAOSTAT: faostat.fao.org
GRAPHICS
FARMING SYSTEMS: FAO Farming Systems and Poverty: www.fao.org/farmingsystems **IRRIGATION:** AQUASTAT, Global Map of Irrigation Areas: http://www.fao.org/nr/water/aquastat/irrigationmap/index.stm **AGRICULTURAL PRODUCTION OVER TIME:** FAOSTAT (available at http://faostat.fao.org/default.aspx) **FISH PRODUCTION OVER TIME:** *FishStat Plus:* www.fao.org/nr/water/aquastat/main/index.stm

Development Indicators pp. 90-91
GENERAL REFERENCES
Central Intelligence Agency (CIA) *The World Factbook,* www.cia.gov; Organisation for Economic Co-operation and Development (OECD): www.oecd.org; World Trade Organization (WTO) International Trade Statistics, 2006.
GRAPHICS
SCHOOL ENROLLMENT: WorldBank.org (Edstats), 2005 **ACCESS TO SANITATION SERVICES:** Millennium Development Goals (UN-MDG); www.un.org/millenniumgoals

World Heritage Sites; Ancient Egypt pp. 92-93
CONSULTANT
Frank Biasi, National Geographic Maps
GENERAL REFERENCE
United Nations Educational, Scientific and Cultural Organization (UNESCO): whc.unesco.org

Suez Canal; Regional History pp. 94-95
GENERAL REFERENCES
Egyptian Maritime Data Bank, http://www.emdb.gov.eg; R.K. Johns & Associates Inc., *Suez Canal Pricing Forecast 2005-2025,* November 2005.

Regional Conflicts pp. 96-97
CONSULTANT
Monty G. Marshall, Center for Systemic Peace and Center for Global Policy, George Mason University
GENERAL REFERENCES
Marshall, Monty G. and Jack Goldstone. *Global Report on Conflict, Governance, and State Fragility, 2007.* Foreign Policy Bulletin 17.1 (Winter 2007): 3-21. (Cambridge University Press Journals). *Proliferation Status 2007* (map). Carnegie Endowment for International Peace. 2005: www.carnegieendowment.org/npp

Israel and the Palestinians pp. 98–99

GENERAL REFERENCES
Lines in the Sand, *National Geographic* magazine, October 2002; United Nations Office for the Coordination of Humanitarian Affairs (UNOCHA), http://ochaopt.org

Iraq pp. 100–101

GENERAL REFERENCES
Compilation by M.R. Izady, based on the following sources: Iraqi news media; US military reports; personal observation; interviews, etc.; United States Army (www.history.army.mil).

GRAPHICS
DISPLACED IRAQIS AROUND THE WORLD: *Statistics on Displaced Iraqis around the World,* September 2007, UNHCR (www.unhcr.org).

Darfur pp. 102–103

CONSULTANT
Alex de Waal, Social Science Research Council

GENERAL REFERENCES
United Nations High Commissioner for Refugees (UNHCR), www.unhcr.org; United Nations Office for the Coordination of Humanitarian Affairs (UNOCHA), http://ochaonline.un.org

Time Line pp. 104–109

CONSULTANT
Michele Dunne, Carnegie Endowment for International Peace

Flags of the Middle East pp. 112–113

CONSULTANT
Whitney Smith, Flag Research Center

KEY TO FACTS

Countries

The National Geographic Society, whose cartographic policy is to recognize de facto countries, counted 193 independent nations as of early 2008. Within the "Countries and Cities" section of the *Atlas of the Middle East*, the 19 independent nations in this region plus the Occupied Palestinian Territories are featured on political maps. Accompanying each map is a table that includes some important statistical data, providing highlights of geography, demography, and economy. These details offer a brief overview of each political entity; they present general characteristics and are not intended to be comprehensive studies. The structured nature of the text results in some generic collective or umbrella terms. The industry category, for instance, includes services in addition to traditional manufacturing sectors. Space limitations dictate the amount of information included. For example, only the most widely spoken languages in each country are listed. The conventional or official long form of the country's name is listed first; if no long form exists, the short form is repeated. Then the flag of each independent nation is shown next to a brief description of the flag and its history.

AREA accounts for the total area of a country, which includes all land and inland water delimited by international boundaries, intranational boundaries, or coastlines. The figures are from the *National Geographic Atlas of the World, 8th edition.*

POPULATION figures for countries are mid-2007 estimates from the 2007 World Population Data Sheet of the Population Reference Bureau, Washington, D.C. Their

web site is www.prb.org. The numbers are rounded to the nearest thousand. Two issues of note: The population of Cyprus shows the number of persons living on the entire island—within both the Republic of Cyprus, and the Turkish Cypriot area in the north. Separate population figures for the West Bank and the Gaza Strip are shown; these are from the Britannica 2007 Book of the Year. The West Bank number includes Jews in settlements.

DEMONYM, or nationality, provides the identifying term for citizens of that country.

CAPITAL gives the name of the seat of government, followed by the city's metropolitan area population, which is from the United Nations Population Division's World Urbanization Prospects: The 2005 Revision: Table A.13, Population of capital cities in 2005. The UN Population Division's web site is: www.un.org/esa/population/unpop.htm. These capital city population figures are rounded to the nearest thousand.

ETHNICITY data are presented in pie charts showing the percentage breakdown of what ethnic groups comprise the people of that country. Data are taken from the CIA's World Factbook; U.S. State Department; *A Dictionary of World History,* Oxford University Press, 2000 (taken from Oxford Reference Online); and the Library of Congress Country Studies.

RELIGION gives the percent of the population who are adherents of the faiths practiced there. Muslims, who are adherents of Islam, make up the greatest percentage for all political entities except for Israel, where a large majority of the population is Jewish and are followers of Judaism, and Cyprus which has a Greek Orthodox majority that are adherents to Christianity. The predominant Muslim sects are shown in rank order in parentheses following the Muslim listing. Data are from the CIA's World Factbook.

LANGUAGE provides a rank order of languages spoken throughout the country. The official language is listed first. It is labeled (official) if space allows, and when there is more than one official language in a country or a language is official in a particular area of a country, this is noted also. Data are from the CIA's World Factbook.

LITERACY generally indicates the percentage of the population above the age of 15 who can read and write. There are no universal standards of literacy, so these estimates (from the CIA's World Factbook) are based on the most common definition available for a nation.

LIFE EXPECTANCY represents the average number of years a newborn infant can expect to live under current mortality levels as defined in the *2007 World Population Data Sheet* of the Population Reference Bureau (PRB).

TROOPS list both active and reserves. Most recent figures are from *The Military Balance: 2007,* International Institute for Strategic Studies.

GDP PER CAPITA is Gross Domestic Product divided by midyear population estimates. GDP estimates are from the CIA's World Factbook 2007. They use the purchasing power parity (PPP) conversion factor designed to equalize the purchasing powers of different currencies. GDP methodology can be found on their web site. Individual income estimates such as GDP PER CAPITA are some of the many indicators used to assess a nation's well-being. But as statistical averages, they hide extremes of poverty and wealth. Furthermore, they take no account of factors that affect quality of life, such as environmental degradation, educational opportunities, and health care. Figures for the West Bank and Gaza Strip are from the UN's Food and Agricultural Organization.

CRUDE OIL RESERVES show in billions of barrels the quantity of crude oil indicated by geological and engineering studies that can be recovered in the future from known underground oil deposits under existing economic and operating conditions. All reserves figures are reported as proved reserves recoverable with current prices and technology. Primary data are Estimated Proved Reserves as of January 1, 2007, from the *International Petroleum Encyclopedia 2007,* Table 1: World Reserves and Production, which uses *Oil & Gas Journal* as its source. Values for Kuwait and Saudi Arabia each include one-half of the reserves in the Neutral Zone.

ECONOMY is divided into three general categories: Industry, Agriculture, and Exports. Because of structural limitations, only the primary industries (IND), agricultural commodities (AGR), and exports (EXP) are reported. Agriculture serves as an umbrella term for not only crops but also livestock products and fish. In the interest of conciseness, agriculture for the independent nations presents, when applicable but not limited to, two major crops, followed respectively by leading entries for livestock products and fish.

AREA COMPARISON: The area of each country is divided by the total area of the 48 contiguous United States, which according to the U.S. Census Bureau is 7,823,315 square kilometers (3,020,560 square miles). Country comparisons with individual states of the U.S. are taken from the CIA's World Factbook and the U.S. State Dept. NA indicates that data are not available. The country shape superimposed over the map of the 48 contiguous U.S. presents a visual comparison of the respective areas of the two countries.

Cities

In the "Countries and Cities" section of this atlas, ten major cities of the Middle East are presented with a map, locator, photograph, and accompanying overview including a paragraph describing the city and its history. As in the countries section, this overview provides general characteristics of each city and is not intended to be a comprehensive study.

POPULATION data are from the United Nations Population Division's World Urbanization Prospects: The 2005 Revision. These numbers are the population of the city's metropolitan area, including any adjacent suburban areas, and are rounded to the nearest thousand.

CITY ELEVATION presents a general average of the elevation of the city, in both meters and feet. The figures do not correspond to a specific point in the respective city.

LATITUDE and **LONGITUDE** give the location of the city rounded to the nearest minute.

TEMPERATURE and **RAINFALL** data are taken from the *National Geographic Concise Atlas of the World, 2nd edition* and the World Meteorological Organization (worldweather.wmo.int). Values in both degrees Celsius and Fahrenheit are given for the average daily high temperature and average daily low temperature for the months of January and July. Average Rainfall values in inches are also given for both of these months.

TIME ZONE shows the difference in hours between local time and Coordinated Universal Time (UTC).

MAJOR INDUSTRIES lists the primary industries in each city, as taken from Encyclopedia Britannica Online and Oxford Reference Online. Industries are listed as space allows, and are not meant to be a comprehensive list of all industries in the city.

PHOTO CREDITS

KEY: LE=Left, RT=Right, CTR=Center, T=Top, B=Bottom, UP=Upper, LO=Lower

COVER: (LE), John Lamb/Getty Images; (LE CTR), NASA; (CTR), Matthieu Colin/Getty Images; (RT CTR), National Geographic Maps; (RT), Paula Bronstein/Getty Images.

4, Mark Horn/Getty Images; 6-7, Paula Bronstein/Getty Images; 8-9 (UP), Graeme Robertson/Getty Images; 9 (LO), Sylvain Grandadam/The Image Bank/Getty Images; 10-11, Lottie Davies/Getty Images; 15 (LE), Atef Safadi/epa/CORBIS; 15 (LE CTR), Asad Zaidi/Bloomberg News/Landov; 15 (CTR), Kazuyoshi Nomachi/CORBIS; 15 (RT CTR), Bagus Indahono/epa/CORBIS; 15 (RT), Gali Tibbon/Pool/epa/CORBIS; 65 (UP), Richard Nowitz/Getty Images; 65 (LO), Steve McCurry/Magnum Photos; 66 (UP), Ramzi Haidar/AFP/Getty Images; 66 (LO), Kenneth Garrett; 67 (UP), Photo by Keith Mellnick; 67 (LO), Andrew Ward/Life File/Getty Images; 68 (UP), Taxi/Getty Images; 68 (LO), Staffan Widstrand/CORBIS; 69 (UP), Mohamed Amin/Camerapix; 69 (LO), Franco Origlia/Getty Images; 71 (LE), Grand Tour/CORBIS; 71 (LE CTR), Claro Cortes IV/Reuters/CORBIS; 71 (CTR), Arthur Thévenart/CORBIS; 71 (RT CTR), Syed Jan Sabawoon/epa/CORBIS; 71 (RT), Goran Tomasevic/Reuters/CORBIS; 79 (UP RT), Preston Schlebusch/Getty Images; 79 (LO RT), Imre Solt; 79 (UP LE), NASA; 79 (LE CTR), NASA; 79 (LO LE), NASA; 89, George Steinmetz/CORBIS; 95 (UP), Imagno/Getty Images; 95 (LO), CORBIS; 99 (UP), AP/Wide World Photos; 99 (CTR), AP/Wide World Photos; 99 (LO), AP/Wide World Photos; 100 (LO LE), AP/Wide World Photos; 100 (LO RT), John Moore/Getty Images; 100 (UP), Hulton-Deutsch Collection/CORBIS; 101 (LO), AP/Wide World Photos; 101 (UP LE), Akram Saleh/Getty Images; 101 (UP CTR), Shepard Sherbell/SABA/CORBIS; 101 (UP RT), David Turnley/CORBIS; 102, Lynsey Addario/CORBIS; 103 (LE), Cris Bouroncle/AFP/Getty Images; 103 (RT), AP/Wide World Photos; 104 (UP LE), Hulton Archive/Getty Images; 104 (UP CTR), Hulton Archive/Getty Images; 104 (UP RT), Hulton Archive/Getty Images; 104 (LO LE), Courtesy Imperial War Museum, London; 104 (LO RT), CORBIS; 105 (UP LE), Hulton Archive/Getty Images; 105 (UP RT), Vittoriano Rastelli/CORBIS; 105 (LO LE), AFP Photo; 105 (LO RT), Hulton-Deutsch Collection/CORBIS; 106 (UP LE), Bettmann/CORBIS; 106 (UP RT), Hulton Archive/Getty Images; 106 (LO LE), CORBIS; 106 (LO RT), Bettmann/CORBIS; 107 (UP LE), Peter Turnley/CORBIS; 107 (UP RT), AFP/CORBIS; 107 (LO LE), Reuters/CORBIS; 107 (LO CTR), AFP Photo/Manoocher Deghati; 107 (LO RT), AFP/Seth McAllister/CORBIS; 108 (UP LE), AP/Wide World Photos; 108 (UP CTR), Ali Haider-Pool/Getty Images; 108 (UP RT), AP/Wide World Photos; 108 (LO LE), AP/Wide World Photos; 108 (LO RT), Shaul Schwarz/CORBIS; 109 (UP LE), Omae Rashidi-Palestinian Authority/epa/CORBIS; 109 (UP RT), AP/Wide World Photos; 109 (LO LE), AP/Wide World Photos; 109 (LO CTR), AP/Wide World Photos; 109 (LO RT), AP/Wide World Photos; 111 (LE), Abedin Taherkenareh/epa/CORBIS; 111 (LE CTR), George Steinmetz/CORBIS; 111 (CTR), Mohamed Messara/epa/CORBIS; 111 (RT CTR), CORBIS; 111 (RT), Construction Photography/CORBIS.

NATIONAL GEOGRAPHIC

Published by the National Geographic Society

John M. Fahey, Jr.
President and Chief Executive Officer

Gilbert M. Grosvenor
Chairman of the Board

Tim T. Kelly
President, Global Media Group

Nina D. Hoffman
Executive Vice President; President, Book Publishing Group

PREPARED BY THE BOOK DIVISION
Kevin Mulroy
Senior Vice President and Publisher

Marianne R. Koszorus
Director of Design

Staff for This Atlas

PROJECT EDITOR AND DIRECTOR OF MAPS
Carl Mehler

MAP EDITORS
Nicholas P. Rosenbach *Supervisor,*
Laura Exner, Steven D. Gardner,
Thomas L. Gray, David B. Miller

MAP RESEARCH
Matt Chwastyk, Steven D. Gardner,
Gregory Ugiansky, and XNR Productions

MAP PRODUCTION MANAGER
Matt Chwastyk

MAP PRODUCTION
John S. Ballay, Steven D. Gardner,
Michael McNey, Tibor G. Tóth,
Gregory Ugiansky, and XNR Productions

SENIOR GEOGRAPHER
David B. Miller

BOOK DESIGN
Marty Ittner

TEXT EDITORS
Victoria Garrett Jones, Judith Klein

PHOTO COORDINATOR
Rob Waymouth

MANAGING EDITOR
Jennifer A. Thornton

PRODUCTION DIRECTOR
Gary Colbert

MANUFACTURING AND QUALITY MANAGEMENT
Christopher A. Liedel
Chief Financial Officer

Phillip L. Schlosser
Vice President

Chris Brown
Director

Since 1888, the National Geographic Society has funded more than 14,000 research, conservation, education, and storytelling projects around the world. National Geographic Partners distributes a portion of the funds it receives from your purchase to National Geographic Society to support programs including the conservation of animals and their habitats.

National Geographic Partners, LLC
1145 17th Street NW
Washington, D.C. 20036-4688 USA

Get closer to National Geographic Explorers and photographers, and connect with our global community. Join us today at nationalgeographic.com/join

For rights or permissions inquiries, please contact National Geographic Books Subsidiary Rights: bookrights@natgeo.com

ISBN: 978-1-4262-0221-6

Printed in Hong Kong
21/PPHK/3